My Journey to Lbsnaa included = Focussed Studies + Discipline + Tapasya + Isolation/Solitude + Coffee (a lot of coffee) 😊

Contents

"Road to LBSNAA: A Comprehensive Guide to Crack UPSC Civil Service IAS Exam":

Introduction:

Ah, the UPSC Civil Services Exam! The Everest of exams, the **Olympics of competitive tests,** the Great Indian Obstacle Course! If you're reading this, it means you've decided to take the plunge into the abyss of books, notes, and unending study hours. Welcome to the madness, my brave friend!

First things first, let's talk about why on earth you would want to become a **civil servant. The glamour? The power?** The ability to sign documents with a flourish? Maybe. But mostly, it's because you have this deep, inexplicable urge to serve the nation, tackle corruption, and, let's face it, the job security isn't bad either!

Now, about this book. It's your trusty guide, your Gandalf in the journey to crack the UPSC exam. **Consider it your best buddy, your BFF,** your personal cheerleader. It will break down the exam into bite-sized chunks, give you tips and tricks, and most importantly, keep you from losing your sanity.

In this first chapter, we'll give you a bird's eye view of the entire UPSC examination process. Think of it as the trailer for a blockbuster movie — all the action, drama, and suspense squeezed into a few pages.

So, sit back, relax (while you still can), and let's embark on this epic journey to LBSNAA – the holy grail for every UPSC aspirant. Get ready to transform from a mere mortal to a mighty IAS officer. The road is long, the path is tough, but with this book in hand, you've got a secret weapon. Let's dive in!

Welcome to the world of UPSC, where coffee is your best friend, and sleep is a distant memory. Let's get started!

The Beginning of Your UPSC Journey

Hello, future IAS officers! So, you've decided to embark on the wild, wonderful, and often wacky journey that is the UPSC exam. Think of it as signing up for the most epic, real-life version of "Survivor." You're about to face a gauntlet of exams, interviews, and study sessions that make Hogwarts look like a summer camp. But don't worry, I'm here to guide you through this maze with humor and practical tips. Let's dive into the introduction – the first chapter of your UPSC saga.

The Call to Adventure

Every hero's journey begins with a call to adventure, and yours is no different. The moment you decide to take on the UPSC, you're essentially saying, "Challenge accepted!"

1. **The Decision:**

   - Deciding to prepare for UPSC is like choosing to climb Mount Everest. It's daunting, but the view from the top is unbeatable.

   - *Example*: Imagine Frodo Baggins deciding to leave the Shire. You're leaving your comfort zone for a quest of epic proportions.

2. **Why UPSC?**

   - Understanding why you're doing this is crucial. Is it the allure of public service? The prestige? The desire to make a difference?

   - *Example*: It's like choosing to become a Jedi. It's not just about the lightsaber; it's about bringing balance to the Force (or society).

3. **Setting the Scene:**

   - Get ready to dive into a world filled with books, notes, and a lot of chai. Your room will soon look like a war room with maps, timelines, and sticky notes.

- o   *Example*: Think of your study space as the Batcave. It's where all your plans and strategies come to life.

Gathering Your Tools

Every hero needs the right tools to succeed. Here's what you need to start your UPSC journey.

1. **Study Material:**

   - o   Collect all the necessary books, notes, and resources. NCERTs, reference books, and previous years' papers are your weapons of choice.

   - o   *Example*: It's like Harry Potter getting his wand and spell books. You need the right tools to cast your knowledge spells.

2. **Coaching Classes:**

   - o   Decide whether you need coaching classes or if you're going to be a self-taught wizard.

   - o   *Example*: Coaching classes are like Dumbledore's Army. You get guidance and support from experienced mentors and fellow aspirants.

3. **Online Resources:**

   - o   Utilize online resources like YouTube channels, educational blogs, and UPSC forums.

   - o   *Example*: The internet is your Marauder's Map. It shows you all the hidden treasures of knowledge.

The Training Begins

Now that you've got your tools, it's time to start training. This is where the real fun begins.

1. **Creating a Study Schedule:**

- o Plan your study schedule meticulously. Balance is key – mix heavy subjects with lighter ones, and don't forget to take breaks.

  - o *Example*: Think of your schedule as a training montage in a Rocky movie. Intense, focused, and inspiring.

2. **Staying Motivated:**

   - o Keep your motivation high by setting small, achievable goals and rewarding yourself when you reach them.

   - o *Example*: Treat yourself like a video game character leveling up. Each milestone is a power-up.

3. **Practice, Practice, Practice:**

   - o Practice writing answers, taking mock tests, and revising regularly.

   - o *Example*: It's like playing Quidditch every day. The more you practice, the better you get at scoring goals (or marks).

The Trials and Tribulations

No hero's journey is complete without facing some trials and tribulations. Here's how to tackle them.

1. **Handling Stress:**

   - o Stress is inevitable, but learning to manage it is crucial. Practice mindfulness, take breaks, and stay connected with friends and family.

   - o *Example*: Think of stress as the dragon Smaug. It seems terrifying, but with the right strategy, you can conquer it.

2. **Dealing with Setbacks:**

   - o You will face setbacks, but don't let them discourage you. Learn from your mistakes and keep moving forward.

   - o *Example*: Setbacks are like the trolls in "The Hobbit." Annoying, but not undefeatable.

3. **Maintaining Balance:**

   o Balance your study time with relaxation and hobbies to avoid burnout.

   o *Example*: It's like being a Jedi. Balance the Force within you by mixing lightsaber practice with meditation.

The Final Battle: Exam Day

The day of the exam is your final battle. Here's how to prepare for it.

1. **Staying Calm:**

   o Keep your nerves in check with deep breathing and positive affirmations.

   o *Example*: Stay calm like Neo in "The Matrix." Believe in yourself and your preparation.

2. **Time Management:**

   o Manage your time wisely during the exam. Allocate time for each section and stick to it.

   o *Example*: Think of it as a timed cooking competition. Every second counts, so don't waste time.

3. **Answer Writing:**

   o Write clear, concise, and well-structured answers. Stick to the point and back up your arguments with facts.

   o *Example*: It's like presenting your dish to the judges in "MasterChef." Make it look good, taste good, and be impressive.

The Aftermath: Results and Beyond

Once the exams are over, it's time to wait for the results and plan your next steps.

1. **Waiting for Results:**

- o Waiting for results can be nerve-wracking, but stay positive and keep yourself occupied.
- o *Example*: It's like waiting for your Hogwarts letter. Patience is key.

2. **Plan B:**

- o Always have a Plan B. If things don't go as expected, be ready to adapt and move forward.
- o *Example*: Think of it as having a backup wand. If one breaks, you have another ready to go.

3. **Stay Positive:**

- o Regardless of the outcome, stay positive and keep striving for your goals.
- o *Example*: Remember, every hero faces setbacks, but it's their resilience that makes them legendary.

Conclusion: Your Heroic Journey

So there you have it, future IAS officers – your humorous and practical guide to the introduction of your UPSC journey. This path is filled with challenges, but with the right attitude, tools, and a pinch of humor, you can navigate it successfully.

1. **Stay Consistent:**

- o Consistency is key. Keep moving forward, no matter what.
- o *Example*: Treat it like brushing your teeth. It's non-negotiable and essential.

2. **Stay Motivated:**

- o Keep your end goal in sight. Visualize your success.
- o *Example*: Create a vision board with inspiring quotes, pictures of LBSNAA, and anything that keeps you motivated.

3. **Stay Positive:**

- o   There will be ups and downs. Stay positive and resilient.

- o   *Example*: Think of yourself as Rocky Balboa – every setback is just a setup for a bigger comeback.

4. **Stay Balanced:**

- o   Balance your studies with relaxation and self-care.

- o   *Example*: All work and no play makes Jack a dull boy. Don't forget to have some fun along the way.

With the right resources, a solid strategy, and a sense of humor, you're all set to embark on this heroic journey to becoming an IAS officer. So, go forth and show the world what you're made of. The road to LBSNAA is tough, but with determination and the right tools, you'll get there. Happy studying and may the force be with you!

Understanding the Syllabus:

Alright, my ambitious friend, it's time to dive into the abyss – the UPSC syllabus. Imagine it as a treasure map, but instead of gold and jewels, the treasure is knowledge (and an IAS badge, which is pretty shiny too).

1. Detailed Syllabus Breakdown:

The syllabus is like a giant pizza with all the toppings you can imagine. Let's slice it up:

- **History**: This isn't just about dates and dead people. It's like binge-watching a historical drama series, where each episode is about epic battles, scandalous betrayals, and, of course, the occasional British guest star.

Example: Know the difference between Ashoka (the guy who turned Buddhist) and Akbar (the guy who turned tolerant). Both were cool in their own ways.

- **Geography**: Think of this as Google Earth on steroids. You need to know everything from the Himalayas to the Deccan Plateau. And yes, you should be able to point them out on a map without using GPS.

Example: "Where is the Thar Desert?" – It's not a new theme park, it's in Rajasthan. And no, it doesn't have a water slide.

- **Polity**: This is like the guidebook to India's political theme park. You'll learn about the Constitution, the Parliament, and why sometimes our politicians behave like they're in a reality TV show.

Example: "What's the difference between Lok Sabha and Rajya Sabha?" – One is like the House of Commons, the other is like the House of Lords, but with more drama and fewer wigs.

- **Economics**: Imagine managing a nation's finances. It's like Monopoly, but with real money and way more complicated rules.

Example: "What is GST?" – It's like that extra charge you see on your pizza bill, but for almost everything you buy.

- **Environment and Ecology**: Think of this as saving the world, one question at a time. You'll learn about conservation, climate change, and why we should care about that one tree in the Amazon rainforest.

Example: "What is an endangered species?" – It's like the unicorns of our planet, except they really exist, and we're trying not to let them go extinct.

- **Science and Technology**: Welcome to the future! Here, you'll get to know about space missions, biotech, and why your smartphone is smarter than your old computer.

Example: "What is ISRO?" – It's like NASA, but with more budget constraints and a lot more jugaad (innovation).

- **Current Affairs**: This is like keeping up with the Kardashians, but way more important. You need to know what's happening in the world, from politics to sports to Nobel prizes.

Example: "Who is the current President of India?" – Always know this. It's like knowing who the principal of your school is.

2. Topic-wise Weightage and Analysis:

Okay, so not every topic is as important as the other. Some are like the main plot, others are just subplots. Focus on the ones that carry more weight. It's like prepping for an exam where you know certain chapters have more marks.

3. Important Areas of Focus:

Your syllabus is vast, like an ocean. But don't worry, you're not alone in this boat. Focus on the critical areas – the icebergs that can either sink your ship or help you reach your destination. Pay extra attention to frequently asked questions, key concepts, and those tricky areas that make you go, "Huh?"

Remember, understanding the syllabus is like getting the cheat codes for a video game. It won't make the game easier, but it will certainly give you an edge. So, grab that map, plot your course, and get ready to conquer the UPSC seas! Happy sailing!

Study Planning and Strategy:

Alright, future IAS officers, buckle up! It's time to craft a master plan, a foolproof strategy, a blueprint for success. Think of it as plotting a heist – but instead of stealing jewels, you're after that coveted UPSC badge. Let's dive into the art of study planning and strategy with a dash of humor and a pinch of practical examples.

Crafting a Study Schedule

Creating a study schedule is like designing your own Hogwarts timetable – except with more books and fewer spells (unfortunately). Here's how you can do it:

1. **Assess Your Strengths and Weaknesses:** Imagine you're a superhero. You need to know your superpowers (strengths) and your kryptonite

(weaknesses). Are you great at history but horrible at economics? Or maybe you can memorize maps but struggle with polity?

Example: If history is your thing, allocate less time to it. If economics makes you want to cry, spend more hours there.

2. **Divide and Conquer:** Break down the syllabus into manageable chunks. Think of it as cutting a giant pizza into slices. No one eats a pizza in one go, right?

Example: Dedicate Monday to history, Tuesday to geography, Wednesday to polity, and so on. Sundays are for revisions and, if you're lucky, Netflix.

3. **Daily and Weekly Goals:** Set achievable goals. Daily goals are like your morning jog – essential but not too taxing. Weekly goals are your marathon – a bit more challenging but totally doable.

Example: Today's goal – read about the Mughal Empire. This week's goal – finish Ancient India. Remember, Rome wasn't built in a day, but they were laying bricks every hour.

Time Management Techniques

Time management is your Excalibur – the sword that will help you slay the UPSC dragon. Let's make sure you wield it wisely.

1. **The Pomodoro Technique:** This technique is a lifesaver. Study for 25 minutes (one Pomodoro) and then take a 5-minute break. Repeat this cycle four times and then take a longer break. It's like interval training for your brain.

Example: Study about the Indian Constitution for 25 minutes. Take a 5-minute break to stretch, grab a coffee, or watch a funny cat video. Rinse and repeat.

2. **Time Blocking:** Allocate specific time blocks for different activities. It's like assigning chores, but for your brain.

Example: 9 AM - 11 AM: Read geography. 11 AM - 11:30 AM: Break. 11:30 AM - 1 PM: Practice CSAT questions. Stick to the schedule like your life depends on it (because it kind of does).

3. **Avoid Multitasking:** Multitasking is like trying to juggle flaming torches while riding a unicycle. Focus on one task at a time. Trust me, your brain will thank you.

Example: If you're reading about Indian polity, don't try to simultaneously solve math problems. One at a time, champ!

Balancing Work, Study, and Personal Life

You're not just a student, you're also a human being (hopefully). Balancing your life is crucial. Here's how to be a UPSC aspirant without turning into a zombie.

1. **Prioritize:** Make a list of your priorities. UPSC prep should be high on the list, but don't forget about eating, sleeping, and occasionally socializing.

Example: If there's a family wedding, it's okay to take a day off. Just don't let it turn into a week-long party binge.

2. **Stay Healthy:** Your body is the temple in which your brain resides. Treat it well. Eat right, sleep enough, and exercise regularly. Think of it as maintenance for your UPSC machine.

Example: Avoid junk food and late-night study marathons. Instead, go for a morning run and stick to a healthy diet. You need your brain cells in peak condition.

3. **Me-Time:** You need time to relax and recharge. Whether it's watching a movie, reading a novel, or just taking a nap, make sure you get some downtime.

Example: Schedule an hour of me-time every day. Use it to do something you love. You're not a robot, after all. (Even though Robot/Machine were the names given to me by some of my friends when I was preparing for this exam ☺)

Effective Note-Making

Notes are your secret weapon. Let's make sure they're sharp and ready for battle.

1. **Keep it Short and Sweet:** Notes should be like a tweet – concise and to the point. Don't write paragraphs when a sentence will do.

Example: Instead of writing "The Battle of Plassey was fought between the British East India Company and the Nawab of Bengal in 1757," write "Plassey: British vs. Bengal, 1757."

2. **Use Bullet Points:** Bullet points are your best friends. They help break down information into bite-sized pieces.

Example:

- Causes of the Revolt of 1857:
    - Economic exploitation
    - Political annexation
    - Social and religious discrimination

3. **Color Coding:** Use different colors for different subjects or importance levels. It's like turning your notes into a visual masterpiece. (Being a colour blind, I can still see some colours and it helped me during prep too, imagine how this would help you!)

Example: Use blue for history, green for geography, and red for important points. Your notes should look like a rainbow of knowledge.

4. **Mind Maps:** Mind maps help visualize connections between topics. It's like drawing a map for your brain.

Example: Create a mind map for the Mauryan Empire. Start with "Mauryan Empire" in the center and branch out into rulers, administration, achievements, etc.

Resources and References

Your study material is your arsenal. Make sure it's stocked with the best weapons.

1. **Recommended Books and Authors:** Stick to the classics. NCERT books are your foundation. Beyond that, pick standard reference books.

Example:

- History: "India's Struggle for Independence" by Bipan Chandra

- o Geography: "Certificate Physical and Human Geography" by Goh Cheng Leong

- o Polity: "Indian Polity" by M. Laxmikanth

2. **Online Resources and Websites:** The internet is a goldmine of resources. Use it wisely.

Example: Websites like Netmock.com and exam.netmock.com (Because I own them) Nextias.com (Because I teach at Next IAS) and The Hindu Newspaper (Because recently got an invite to write for it) can be used. **[Total blatant promotion 😊]**

3. **Coaching Institutes:** Coaching can help, but it's not a magic wand. Choose wisely and don't rely solely on them.

Example: Institutes like NextIAS (Because it is the best!) can provide you an excellent platform. But remember, self-study is crucial. For online Courses you can enrol in my course on exam.netmock.com, and you can use the coupon exclusively for this book readers **Book20** for 20% discount. See, how smoothly I am promoting my course. You also need **to learn the art of writing to sell your answers to the answer checker** to get more marks.

4. **Mock Tests and Previous Years' Papers:** These are your practice rounds. The more you solve, the better prepared you'll be.

Example: Solve at least one mock test every week. Review your answers, understand your mistakes, and improve.

Preliminary Examination Preparation

Prelims are your first hurdle. Here's how to ace it.

1. **Strategies for General Studies Paper I:** This paper is vast. Cover all subjects but focus on your strengths.

Example: If you're good at geography, ensure you get all geography questions right. For weaker areas, aim for a decent score.

2. **Tips for CSAT Paper II:** CSAT is qualifying but don't take it lightly. Practice logical reasoning, math, and comprehension regularly.

Example: Solve CSAT papers from previous years. Time yourself and analyze your performance.

3. **Solving Objective Type Questions:** Objective questions require precision. Practice makes perfect.

Example: Use elimination techniques to narrow down options. Guess only if you're reasonably sure – negative marking can be a killer.

4. **Practice and Revision Techniques:** Regular revision is key. It's like watering a plant – do it often, and your knowledge will bloom.

Example: Revise weekly. Use flashcards, quizzes, and short notes to keep information fresh in your mind.

Main Examination Preparation

The mains are your marathon. Train hard, run smart.

1. **Writing High-Quality Essays:** Essays are your chance to shine. Make them count.

Example: Practice writing essays on diverse topics. Structure them well with an introduction, body, and conclusion. Use quotes and examples to enrich your content.

2. **Tackling General Studies Papers:** Each paper has its own challenges. Be ready.

    o   **Indian Heritage and Culture, History, and Geography:**

        ▪   Cover ancient to modern history. Know cultural landmarks.

        ▪   Understand geographical concepts and their applications.

    o   **Governance, Constitution, Polity, Social Justice, and International Relations:**

        ▪   Focus on constitutional provisions, governance issues, and key international bodies.

Example: Knowing the capitals of countries or the rivers in India is like knowing the main characters in a soap opera. You can't follow the plot if you don't know who's who.

4. **Reading NCERTs:** NCERT books are your old, trusted friends. They might seem boring, but they hold all the secrets.

Example: Reading NCERTs is like watching "Friends" reruns. You've seen it before, but every time you watch, you find something new and useful.

5. **Making Notes:** Notes are your personal cheat sheets. Keep them concise and to the point.

Example: Think of making notes as creating a highlights reel of a sports match. You don't need every detail, just the important plays.

Tips for CSAT Paper II

CSAT (Civil Services Aptitude Test) is like the UPSC's way of saying, "Let's see how clever you really are." It's qualifying but crucial.

1. **Comprehension:** Reading comprehension is like deciphering a complex plot twist. Take your time and understand the passage.

Example: Imagine you're Sherlock Holmes solving a mystery. Pay attention to every detail in the passage to find the right answers.

2. **Logical Reasoning:** Logical reasoning is like solving a puzzle. It tests your ability to think clearly and logically.

Example: Picture yourself as a contestant on "The Crystal Maze," figuring out how to escape a locked room using clues. That's logical reasoning for you.

3. **Quantitative Aptitude:** Don't panic; it's not as scary as it sounds. Brush up on your basic math skills.

Example: Think of quantitative aptitude as counting your pocket money or calculating discounts while shopping. It's just a bit more formal.

4. **Practice Regularly:** Consistent practice is key. The more you practice, the better you get.

Example: Practicing CSAT questions is like going to the gym. The more you work out, the stronger you get. Don't skip leg day or quant day!

Solving Objective Type Questions

Objective questions are tricky little creatures. Here's how to tame them.

1. **Read the Questions Carefully:** Sometimes, the trickiest part is understanding the question.

Example: It's like reading the fine print in a contract. You need to know exactly what's being asked before you can answer correctly.

2. **Elimination Method:** If you're unsure, eliminate the obviously wrong answers first.

Example: Think of it as a multiple-choice game show. Knock out the wrong answers to increase your chances of winning the grand prize.

3. **Avoid Negative Marking:** Guess only if you're reasonably sure. Wild guesses can hurt your score.

Example: It's like playing Russian roulette. You don't want to take unnecessary risks that could backfire.

4. **Time Management:** Don't spend too much time on any one question. Move on and come back if you have time.

Example: Imagine you're on a cooking show with a time limit. If one dish isn't working out, move on to the next and come back later if you can.

Practice and Revision Techniques

Practice and revision are your bread and butter. Here's how to keep them fresh.

1. **Regular Practice:** Make practice a daily habit. Consistency is key.

Example: Treat your studies like brushing your teeth. You wouldn't skip a day, would you?

2. **Mock Tests:** Take mock tests to simulate the exam environment.

Example: Think of mock tests as dress rehearsals for a play. The more you rehearse, the more confident you'll be on the big day.

3. **Review Mistakes:** Go over your mistakes to understand where you went wrong.

Example: Imagine you're a football coach reviewing game footage. Understanding your mistakes is the first step to improving your performance.

4. **Revise Regularly:** Keep revising your notes and key concepts.

Example: Revision is like watering your plants. Do it regularly, and your knowledge will bloom.

Balancing Preparation with Relaxation

You're not a study robot. You need breaks to keep your brain fresh.

1. **Take Short Breaks:** Use the Pomodoro Technique – 25 minutes of study followed by a 5-minute break.

Example: Think of it as interval training for your brain. Short, intense bursts followed by recovery time.

2. **Stay Active:** Physical activity can boost your brain power.

Example: Go for a walk, do some yoga, or dance like nobody's watching. Get those endorphins flowing!

3. **Stay Social:** Don't become a hermit. Spend time with friends and family.

Example: Think of social interactions as mental spa days. They refresh and recharge you.

4. **Sleep Well:** Don't sacrifice sleep for study. Your brain needs rest to function properly.

Example: Sleeping well is like rebooting your computer. It clears out the junk and helps you run smoothly.

Making the Most of Study Groups

Study groups can be a great way to learn and stay motivated.

1. **Choose Your Group Wisely:** Pick study buddies who are serious and committed.

Example: Think of your study group as the Fellowship of the Ring. Everyone should be focused on the same goal.

2. **Divide and Conquer:** Split topics among group members and teach each other.

Example: It's like potluck dinners. Everyone brings something to the table, and you all benefit.

3. **Regular Meetings:** Schedule regular study sessions to stay on track.

Example: Treat your study group like a weekly book club. Regular meetings keep everyone accountable.

4. **Stay Focused:** Don't let study sessions turn into gossip sessions.

Example: Imagine you're a team of superheroes planning a mission. Stay focused on the task at hand.

Using Technology to Your Advantage

Tech can be a powerful ally in your UPSC prep.

1. **Online Courses:** Enroll in online courses for structured learning.

Example: Think of online courses as your personal Yoda – guiding you through the UPSC Force.

2. **Educational Apps:** Use apps for quizzes, flashcards, and current affairs.

Example: Educational apps are like the Pokémon Go of learning. Fun, interactive, and informative.

3. **YouTube:** Watch lectures and explainer videos.

Example: YouTube is like having a library of TED Talks at your fingertips. Use it wisely.

4. **Digital Notes:** Use apps like Evernote or OneNote to keep your notes organized.

Example: Digital notes are like having a magical notebook that never runs out of pages and is always accessible.

Staying Motivated Throughout Your Preparation

UPSC prep is a marathon, not a sprint. Stay motivated.

1. **Set Small Goals:** Break your big goal into smaller, manageable chunks.

Example: Think of it as climbing a mountain. Focus on reaching the next base camp rather than the summit.

2. **Celebrate Milestones:** Reward yourself for achieving small goals.

Example: Treat yourself to an episode of your favorite show or a scoop of ice cream when you complete a study milestone.

3. **Stay Positive:** Keep a positive mindset. Believe in yourself.

Example: Imagine yourself as Rocky Balboa. Every setback is just another step towards a comeback.

4. **Visualize Success:** Picture yourself as an IAS officer. Let that image motivate you.

Example: Create a vision board with pictures of LBSNAA, inspirational quotes, and anything that reminds you of your goal.

Managing Exam Day Nerves

The big day is here. Stay calm and composed.

1. **Be Prepared:** Pack your bag with all necessary items the night before.

Example: Think of it as packing for a vacation. Make sure you have everything you need to avoid last-minute stress.

2. **Stay Positive:** Keep a positive mindset. Visualize success.

Example: Imagine you're Harry Potter about to face Voldemort. Believe in your training and abilities.

3. **Time Management:** Keep an eye on the clock during the exam.

Example: Think of it as a timed cooking challenge on "MasterChef." Pace yourself to ensure you finish all the dishes (questions).

4. **Stay Calm:** Take deep breaths and stay calm if you encounter a tough question.

Example: Picture yourself as a Zen master. Breathe in, breathe out, and tackle the question with a clear mind.

Post-Exam Strategies

The exam is over. Now what?

1. **Relax:** Take a well-deserved break. Relax and recharge.

Example: Treat yourself to a mini-vacation or a Netflix binge. You've earned it.

2. **Analyze Performance:** Reflect on your performance. Identify strengths and areas for improvement.

Example: Think of it as a post-match analysis. Understand what went well and where you can do better.

3. **Prepare for Mains:** If you think you did well, start preparing for the mains immediately.

Example: It's like winning a qualifying round. Gear up for the finals without losing momentum.

4. **Stay Updated:** Keep an eye on the results announcement. Stay informed.

Example: Follow the UPSC website and relevant forums like a hawk. Don't miss any updates.

Conclusion: Your Roadmap to Prelims Success

So, there you have it, future IAS officers – your comprehensive, humorous guide to cracking the UPSC Preliminary Examination. Remember, this journey is long and demanding, but with the right strategies, a positive mindset, and a bit of humor, you can navigate it successfully.

1. **Stay Consistent:** Consistency is the key to success. Study every day, even if it's just for a few hours.

Example: Treat your study schedule like a daily workout. You wouldn't skip a day, would you?

2. **Stay Motivated:** Keep your end goal in sight. Visualize yourself as an IAS officer.

Example: Create a vision board with inspiring quotes, pictures of LBSNAA, and anything that keeps you motivated.

3. **Stay Positive:** There will be ups and downs. Stay positive and resilient.

Example: Think of yourself as Rocky Balboa – every setback is just a setup for a bigger comeback.

4. **Stay Balanced:** Balance your studies with relaxation and self-care.

Example: All work and no play make Jack a dull boy. Don't forget to have some fun along the way.

With the right resources, a solid strategy, and a pinch of humor, you're all set to conquer the UPSC Prelims. So, go forth and show the world what you're made of. The road to LBSNAA is tough, but with determination and the right tools, you'll get there. Happy studying!

Main Examination Preparation: Developing Answer Writing Skills:

Hello, future IAS officers! You've been studying hard, cramming facts into your brain like a human encyclopedia, and now it's time to master the art of answer writing. Think of it as being a master chef who can whip up a gourmet dish under pressure. Your answers need to be clear, concise, and compelling. Let's dive into this culinary adventure with humor and practical tips to make your answer writing skills sizzle.

Understanding the Recipe: The Structure of a Good Answer

Just like a delicious meal has a recipe, a good answer has a structure. Here's the secret sauce:

1. **Introduction:**

    o   Start with a brief introduction to set the stage.

    o   *Example*: Think of your introduction as the appetizer. It should be light and engaging, making the reader want more.

2. **Body:**

    o   The body is where you present your main arguments, evidence, and analysis.

    o   *Example*: This is the main course. Each paragraph is like a different dish, contributing to the overall feast.

3. **Conclusion:**

    o   End with a concise conclusion that summarizes your points and provides closure.

    o   *Example*: The conclusion is the dessert – sweet, satisfying, and leaving a good taste in the examiner's mouth.

Whipping Up the Introduction

Your introduction sets the tone for the rest of your answer. Make it count.

1. **Start with a Hook:**

    o   Use an interesting fact, quote, or question to grab attention.

    o   *Example*: Think of it as a splash of lime in your drink. It wakes up the taste buds and gets the party started.

2. **Provide Context:**

    o   Briefly introduce the topic and its significance.

- o *Example*: Imagine you're setting the table before serving the meal. The context helps the examiner understand what's coming.

3. **State Your Thesis:**

   - o Clearly state your main argument or the purpose of your answer.

   - o *Example*: The thesis is like the menu for the evening. It tells your guests (the examiner) what to expect.

Cooking Up the Body

The body is where you showcase your knowledge and analytical skills.

1. **Paragraph Structure:**

   - o Each paragraph should have a clear main idea, supporting evidence, and a conclusion.

   - o *Example*: Think of each paragraph as a layered cake. The main idea is the base, the evidence is the filling, and the conclusion is the icing.

2. **Use Examples:**

   - o Real-life examples make your arguments more relatable and convincing.

   - o *Example*: Examples are like spices. They add flavor and make the dish more interesting.

3. **Connect Your Ideas:**

   - o Ensure your paragraphs flow logically from one to the next.

   - o *Example*: It's like arranging a multi-course meal. Each dish should complement the others, not clash with them.

4. **Be Concise:**

   - o Stick to the point and avoid unnecessary details.

- o *Example*: Conciseness is like reducing a sauce. You want to keep the essence without the excess liquid.

Crafting a Delicious Conclusion

Your conclusion should wrap up your answer neatly.

1. **Summarize Key Points:**

    - o Briefly recap the main arguments of your answer.

    - o *Example*: Think of it as the final course. It should remind the examiner of the highlights of the meal.

2. **Restate Your Thesis:**

    - o Reinforce your main argument in light of the evidence presented.

    - o *Example*: The conclusion is like the final toast. It brings everything together and leaves a lasting impression.

3. **End with a Bang:**

    - o Leave the reader with something to ponder or a call to action.

    - o *Example*: A memorable conclusion is like a chocolate mint at the end of the meal. It's a small touch, but it leaves a great impression.

The Spice Rack: Adding Flavor to Your Answers

Adding "spices" can make your answers stand out.

1. **Use Quotes and Anecdotes:**

    - o Relevant quotes and anecdotes can add depth to your answer.

    - o *Example*: Quotes are like a dash of truffle oil – rich and elevating the dish.

2. **Incorporate Data and Statistics:**

    - o Use data to back up your arguments.

- o *Example*: Data is like the seasoning – it needs to be balanced, not overpowering.

3. **Visual Aids:**

   - o Diagrams, charts, and tables can make your answer more appealing.

   - o *Example*: Visual aids are like garnish – they make the dish look attractive and enhance the overall experience.

4. **Use Clear Language:**

   - o Avoid jargon and use simple, clear language.

   - o *Example*: Clear language is like using fresh ingredients – it makes everything taste better.

Practice Makes Perfect: Regular Writing Practice

Practice is the key to mastering answer writing.

1. **Daily Writing Practice:**

   - o Write answers daily to improve your skills.

   - o *Example*: Think of it as your daily cooking practice. The more you cook, the better you get.

2. **Time Yourself:**

   - o Practice writing answers within a set time limit.

   - o *Example*: Timing yourself is like participating in a cooking show. You need to be quick and efficient.

3. **Review and Revise:**

   - o Review your answers and revise them to improve.

   - o *Example*: Revising is like tasting and adjusting your dish. It's crucial for perfection.

4. **Seek Feedback:**

   o   Get feedback from peers, mentors, or teachers.

   o   *Example*: Feedback is like a taste test. It helps you identify what's working and what needs improvement.

Avoiding Common Pitfalls: What Not to Do

Be aware of common mistakes that can spoil your answer.

1. **Going Off-Topic:**

   o   Stick to the question and avoid unnecessary tangents.

   o   *Example*: Going off-topic is like adding too many random ingredients. It confuses the flavor.

2. **Overloading with Facts:**

   o   Don't overwhelm the reader with too many facts. Focus on analysis and insights.

   o   *Example*: Too many facts are like too much salt. It ruins the dish.

3. **Ignoring Structure:**

   o   A well-structured answer is easier to read and understand.

   o   *Example*: Structure is like the backbone of your dish. Without it, everything falls apart.

4. **Repetition:**

   o   Avoid repeating the same points. Be concise and varied in your arguments.

   o   *Example*: Repetition is like serving the same course twice. It gets boring quickly.

Using Humor Effectively: Lighten Up Your Answers

Humor can make your answers more engaging, but use it wisely.

1. **Be Subtle:**

    o   Use humor subtly to keep it professional.

    o   *Example*: Subtle humor is like a hint of lemon zest – it adds a refreshing touch without overpowering the dish.

2. **Relevance:**

    o   Ensure your humor is relevant to the topic.

    o   *Example*: Relevant humor is like pairing wine with food. It enhances the experience.

3. **Balance:**

    o   Don't overdo it. Balance humor with serious analysis.

    o   *Example*: Humor is like a pinch of chili – a little goes a long way.

The Final Presentation: Making Your Answers Shine

Presentation matters. Make your answers look as good as they taste.

1. **Neat Handwriting:**

    o   Write neatly and legibly.

    o   *Example*: Neat handwriting is like plating a dish beautifully. It's the first thing the examiner sees.

2. **Proper Formatting:**

    o   Use proper headings, bullet points, and paragraphs.

    o   *Example*: Formatting is like arranging your ingredients. It makes the preparation smoother and the final dish more appealing.

3. **Highlight Key Points:**

    o   Use underlining or highlighting to draw attention to important points.

- *Example*: Highlighting key points is like adding a garnish. It draws the eye to the best parts of the dish.

4. **Leave Space:**

   - Leave space between answers to make them more readable.

   - *Example*: Leaving space is like not overcrowding the plate. It looks more appealing and is easier to navigate.

Sample Answer: A Culinary Example

Let's put it all together with a sample answer. Here's a mock question and answer to illustrate the principles we've discussed.

Question: Discuss the impact of climate change on agriculture and suggest measures to mitigate its effects.

Introduction: Climate change is like a stubborn stain on the fabric of our planet, affecting every aspect of our lives, especially agriculture. With rising temperatures, unpredictable rainfall, and extreme weather events, farmers are finding it increasingly difficult to maintain their livelihoods.

Body: Impact on Agriculture:

1. **Crop Yields:**

   - Higher temperatures and altered rainfall patterns are reducing crop yields.

   - *Example*: It's like trying to bake bread in a faulty oven – inconsistent results and often disappointing.

2. **Soil Degradation:**

   - Extreme weather events cause soil erosion and degradation.

   - *Example*: Imagine making a cake with expired ingredients – it just doesn't hold up.

3. **Pest and Disease:**

   - Warmer climates favor the proliferation of pests and diseases.

- o *Example*: It's like leaving your food out in the open – pests get to it before you do.

Measures to Mitigate Effects:

1. **Climate-Resilient Crops:**
   - o Developing and planting climate-resilient crop varieties.
   - o *Example*: Think of it as using hardy ingredients that can withstand a variety of cooking conditions.

2. **Sustainable Farming Practices:**
   - o Adopting sustainable farming practices like crop rotation and organic farming.
   - o *Example*: Sustainable farming is like using eco-friendly cookware – better for the environment and your health.

3. **Technological Innovations:**
   - o Utilizing technology for precision farming and weather forecasting.
   - o *Example*: Technology in farming is like using a smart kitchen appliance – efficient and effective.

Conclusion: Climate change poses significant challenges to agriculture, but with the right measures, we can mitigate its effects. By adopting climate-resilient crops, sustainable practices, and technological innovations, we can ensure food security for future generations. Just as a master chef adapts to available ingredients and kitchen conditions, farmers must adapt to the changing climate to sustain their livelihoods.

Conclusion: Your Culinary Journey to Mastering Answer Writing

So there you have it, future IAS officers – your comprehensive, humorous guide to developing answer writing skills. This journey is demanding, but with the right strategies, a positive mindset, and a bit of humor, you can master it successfully.

1. **Stay Consistent:**

- o Consistency is key. Practice regularly and stay committed.

- o *Example*: Treat it like brushing your teeth. It's non-negotiable and essential.

2. **Stay Motivated:**

   - o Keep your end goal in sight. Visualize your success.

   - o *Example*: Create a vision board with inspiring quotes, pictures of LBSNAA, and anything that keeps you motivated.

3. **Stay Positive:**

   - o There will be ups and downs. Stay positive and resilient.

   - o *Example*: Think of yourself as Rocky Balboa – every setback is just a setup for a bigger comeback.

4. **Stay Balanced:**

   - o Balance your studies with relaxation and self-care.

   - o *Example*: All work and no play makes Jack a dull boy. Don't forget to have some fun along the way.

With the right resources, a solid strategy, and a pinch of humor, you're all set to become a master of answer writing. So, go forth and show the world what you're made of. The road to LBSNAA is tough, but with determination and the right tools, you'll get there. Happy studying and happy writing!

Personality Test (Interview) Preparation:

Alright, future bureaucrats, you've made it through the prelims and the mains. Now it's time for the final boss level: the Personality Test, also known as the interview. Imagine this as the final showdown in a reality TV show where the judges are serious, the stakes are high, and the spotlight is on you. Let's dive into how to prepare for this with humor, examples, and practical advice.

Understanding the Interview Process

The interview is like a sophisticated job interview crossed with a talent show. The panel wants to see if you're not just book-smart but also street-smart, confident, and grounded.

1. **The Panel:** The interview panel usually consists of senior bureaucrats and experts. Think of them as a mix of Simon Cowell (brutally honest), Gordon Ramsay (demanding), and Oprah (empathetic).

Example: Picture yourself in front of a panel that might ask you about your opinion on global warming, your hobbies, and why you think pineapple on pizza is a travesty.

2. **Duration:** The interview typically lasts 20-30 minutes. It's like the grand finale of a cooking show – short but intense.

Example: In those 20-30 minutes, you need to be as engaging as a TED talk and as concise as a tweet.

3. **Purpose:** They assess your personality, attitude, and suitability for a career in public service.

Example: It's like a beauty pageant but for brains and character. You need to show you're not just a pretty face (or a walking encyclopedia) but someone with the right attitude and integrity.

Commonly Asked Questions

Expect a variety of questions that test your knowledge, personality, and presence of mind. Here's how to tackle some typical ones:

1. **Tell us about yourself:** This is your chance to set the stage. Keep it concise and highlight relevant aspects of your life.

Example: "I'm [Your Name], a graduate in [Your Field] from [Your University]. I'm passionate about public service and have been actively involved in [mention any relevant activities]. In my free time, I enjoy [your hobbies]."

2. **Why do you want to join the civil services?** Be honest and articulate your motivation clearly.

Example: "I want to join the civil services because I believe in the power of good governance to bring about social change. I want to be a part of the solution to our country's challenges."

3. **Current Affairs:** Stay updated with the latest news. You might be asked for your opinion on recent events.

Example: "The recent climate summit highlighted the urgency of addressing global warming. I believe India's role is crucial in leading sustainable development initiatives."

4. **Situational Questions:** These test your decision-making and ethical values.

Example: "If you were a district collector and faced with a flood crisis, how would you prioritize rescue operations?"

5.   **Hobbies and Interests:** Be prepared to talk about your hobbies in detail.

Example: If you say you like reading, be ready to discuss your favorite book and its impact on you. "I enjoy reading historical fiction, and 'The Nightingale' by Kristin Hannah deeply moved me with its portrayal of resilience during World War II."

Developing Communication Skills

Your communication skills are crucial. You need to be clear, concise, and confident.

1.   **Practice Speaking:** Practice speaking in front of a mirror or with friends.

Example: Imagine you're giving a TED talk about yourself. Engage your audience with eye contact and clear articulation.

2.   **Body Language:** Your body language speaks volumes. Sit straight, make eye contact, and avoid fidgeting.

Example: Think of yourself as a news anchor – poised, professional, and confident.

3.   **Clarity and Brevity:** Be clear and to the point. Don't ramble.

Example: If asked about your opinion on a policy, get straight to the point. "I believe the policy is effective because it addresses the core issue of unemployment by providing skill development programs."

Mock Interviews and Feedback

Mock interviews are your rehearsal for the big day. The more you practice, the better.

1.   **Join a Coaching Institute:** Many coaching institutes offer mock interview sessions.

Example: Treat these sessions like dress rehearsals for a play. The feedback you get is invaluable.

2.   **Peer Group Practice:** Conduct mock interviews with friends.

Example: Turn it into a fun activity. Have your friends play the roles of stern interviewers. It's like a friendly roast but for serious prep.

3.   **Record and Review:** Record your practice interviews and review them.

Example: Watching yourself on video helps you catch any nervous habits or unclear answers. It's like watching game footage to improve your performance.

Handling Stress and Nervousness

Everyone gets nervous. The trick is to manage it.

1. **Deep Breathing:** Practice deep breathing exercises to stay calm.

Example: Think of deep breathing as your secret weapon – like a Jedi using the Force to stay calm and focused.

2. **Positive Visualization:** Visualize yourself succeeding in the interview.

Example: Picture the panel smiling and nodding at your brilliant answers. It's like creating a mental movie of your success.

3. **Stay Hydrated:** Drink water to stay hydrated and calm.

Example: Water is like your magic potion. It keeps you cool and composed.

4. **Relaxation Techniques:** Use relaxation techniques like meditation or yoga.

Example: Think of meditation as your mental spa day – it helps clear your mind and reduce anxiety.

Dressing the Part

Your appearance matters. Dress professionally and comfortably.

1. **Formal Attire:** Wear formal attire that's comfortable and fits well.

Example: Think of it as dressing for a royal ball. You want to look sharp and feel comfortable.

2. **Grooming:** Pay attention to grooming. Neat hair and clean nails are a must.

Example: It's like preparing for a photo shoot. Every detail counts.

3. **Minimal Accessories:** Keep accessories to a minimum. They should enhance, not distract.

Example: Think of accessories as the icing on the cake. A little is good, but too much can be overwhelming.

Showcasing Your Personality

Your personality is what makes you unique. Let it shine.

1. **Be Genuine:** Be yourself. Authenticity is key.

Example: Think of the interview as a friendly chat. You're not acting; you're showcasing your best self.

2. **Stay Humble:** Be confident but not arrogant.

Example: It's like being a superhero – strong but humble. Think of yourself as Captain America, not Tony Stark.

3. **Show Enthusiasm:** Let your passion for public service show.

Example: Imagine you're talking about your favorite hobby. Let that same enthusiasm come through when you talk about joining the civil services.

4. **Be Positive:** Maintain a positive attitude throughout the interview.

Example: Think of yourself as a ray of sunshine on a cloudy day. Your positivity can brighten the room.

Handling Tricky Questions

Tricky questions are designed to test your composure and thinking.

1. **Stay Calm:** Take a moment to think before answering.

Example: If asked a tough question, take a deep breath and think of it as a puzzle. Solve it piece by piece.

2. **Be Honest:** If you don't know the answer, it's okay to admit it.

Example: "I'm not sure about the specifics, but I would research thoroughly and consult experts to make an informed decision."

3. **Think Aloud:** Explain your thought process.

Example: If asked about solving a complex issue, outline your approach. "First, I would gather data, then analyze the root causes, and finally implement a strategic plan."

4. **Stay Positive:** Turn tricky questions into opportunities to showcase your strengths.

Example: If asked about a failure, focus on what you learned. "I faced a setback in my project, but it taught me resilience and the importance of teamwork."

Preparing for the Big Day

The interview day is here. Be ready.

1. **Get a Good Night's Sleep:** Rest well the night before.

Example: Think of it as recharging your batteries. You need full power for the big day.

2. **Eat a Healthy Breakfast:** Have a nutritious breakfast to fuel your brain.

Example: Breakfast is your power-up potion. It keeps you energized and focused.

3. **Arrive Early:** Arrive at the venue early to avoid any last-minute stress.

Example: It's like catching a flight. Better to be early and relaxed than rushed and anxious.

4. **Stay Positive:** Keep a positive mindset. You've prepared well.

Example: Imagine yourself as a gladiator entering the arena. You're ready for whatever comes your way.

Conclusion: Your Roadmap to Interview Success

So there you have it, future IAS officers – your comprehensive, humorous guide to acing the UPSC Personality Test. Remember, this journey is challenging but incredibly rewarding. With the right preparation, a positive mindset, and a bit of humor, you can navigate the interview successfully.

1. **Stay Consistent:** Consistency is key. Practice regularly and stay committed.

Example: Treat your preparation like training for a marathon. Every step counts.

2. **Stay Motivated:** Keep your goal in sight. Visualize your success.

Example: Create a vision board with inspiring quotes, pictures of LBSNAA, and anything that keeps you motivated.

3. **Stay Positive:** There will be ups and downs. Stay positive and resilient.

Example: Think of yourself as Rocky Balboa – every setback is just a setup for a bigger comeback.

4. **Stay Balanced:** Balance your preparation with relaxation and self-care.

Example: All work and no play makes Jack a dull boy. Don't forget to have some fun along the way.

With the right resources, a solid strategy, and a pinch of humor, you're all set to conquer the UPSC interview. So, go forth and show the world what you're made of. The road to LBSNAA is tough, but with determination and the right tools, you'll get there. Happy preparing!

Current Affairs and General Knowledge:

Hello, future officers! You've tackled the prelims and the mains, and now it's time to dive deep into the ocean of current affairs and general knowledge. Think of it as preparing for a grand quiz show where every question counts, and your grasp of the latest happenings can make or break your score. Let's embark on this journey with a sprinkle of humor and some practical tips.

Staying Updated with News

Staying updated with current affairs is like keeping up with a never-ending season of your favorite TV show. You need to know who did what, where, and why. Here's how to make it fun and effective.

1. **Daily News Reading:** Reading the newspaper should be a daily ritual. Pick a reliable newspaper like **The Hindu or The Indian Express.**

Example: Imagine you're Sherlock Holmes and the newspaper is your Watson, providing you with all the clues to solve the mystery of current affairs.

2. **Digital News Platforms:** Use apps like Inshorts or Flipboard to get quick updates.

Example: Think of these apps as your morning coffee – a quick shot of news to jumpstart your day.

3. **TV News Channels:** Watch news channels like Rajya Sabha TV or Lok Sabha TV (Now, Sansad TV) for detailed discussions and analyses.

Example: It's like attending a live debate club where experts dissect every issue with surgical precision.

4. **News Websites:** Follow reliable news websites like Newsonair.nic.in, Sansad TV

Example: Consider these websites as your global news buffet – a little bit of everything from around the world.

Analyzing Current Affairs

Understanding news is not just about knowing what happened but also why it happened and what it means. Let's break it down.

1. **Contextual Understanding:** Always try to understand the background of the news.

Example: If a new economic policy is announced, understand the existing economic scenario that led to this decision. It's like knowing the backstory of a superhero – it makes their actions more meaningful.

2. **Cause and Effect:** Identify the causes and consequences of events.

Example: Think of it as a domino effect. One event leads to another, and understanding this chain reaction can give you deeper insights.

3. **Connecting the Dots:** Relate current events to historical or geographical contexts.

Example: It's like playing a giant game of connect-the-dots. Each news story is a dot, and connecting them gives you the bigger picture.

4. **Critical Thinking:** Question and analyze the news critically.

Example: Don't take everything at face value. Be like an investigative journalist digging for the truth behind the headlines.

Importance of Magazines and Newspapers

Magazines and newspapers provide in-depth analysis and comprehensive coverage of current affairs.

1. **Yojana and Kurukshetra:** These government publications offer insights into socio-economic issues and government schemes.

Example: Think of them as detailed study guides written by experts – your secret weapons for understanding complex topics.

2. **Economic and Political Weekly (EPW):** EPW provides scholarly articles on various socio-economic issues.

Example: It's like reading research papers without the boring jargon – in-depth, insightful, and informative.

3. **Monthly Current Affairs Magazines:** Any Magazine of your choice.

Example: These magazines are like your monthly bullet journal – summarizing everything important that happened.

Using Mobile Apps and Online Resources

Harness the power of technology to stay updated and revise efficiently.

1. **Current Affairs Apps:** Use apps like NetmockIAS (More Promotion) for daily current affairs updates.

Example: These apps are like having a personal tutor in your pocket, guiding you through the maze of current events.

2. **Online Forums:** Participate in discussions on forums like Quora or Reddit.

Example: It's like joining a global study group where you can discuss and debate various topics with peers.

3. **YouTube Channels:** Follow YouTube channels dedicated to UPSC preparation for video lectures and discussions.

Example: Think of these channels as your online classroom – visual and interactive learning at its best.

4. **Podcasts:** Listen to news podcasts while commuting or exercising.

Example: It's like having a news radio station that plays only the tracks you're interested in.

Creating a Study Schedule for Current Affairs

A structured approach to studying current affairs can save you time and effort.

1. **Daily Routine:** Dedicate a specific time each day to read the news.

Example: Make it part of your morning routine, like brushing your teeth. A cup of coffee, a newspaper, and you're ready to conquer the day.

2. **Weekly Reviews:** Summarize and review the week's major news stories every Sunday.

Example: Think of it as a weekly wrap-up show where you recap all the highlights.

3. **Monthly Compilation:** Create monthly notes summarizing the key events and issues.

Example: It's like creating a scrapbook of current affairs – concise, organized, and easy to review.

4. **Thematic Study:** Focus on different themes each week, such as economy, environment, or international relations.

Example: Imagine you're a chef preparing different dishes each week. Each theme is a new recipe to master.

Making Notes Effectively

Good notes are crucial for quick revision and retention.

1. **Concise and Clear:** Keep your notes short and to the point.

Example: Think of your notes as tweets – informative yet concise.

2. **Use Bullet Points:** Bullet points make notes easy to read and remember.

Example: Imagine your notes are a grocery list – simple, clear, and organized.

3. **Visual Aids:** Use diagrams, charts, and mind maps to visualize information.

Example: It's like adding illustrations to a storybook – making it more engaging and easier to understand.

4. **Regular Updates:** Update your notes regularly to keep them current.

Example: Treat your notes like a living document. They grow and evolve with each new piece of information.

Revising Current Affairs

Regular revision is key to retaining information.

1. **Daily Revision:** Review your notes daily to reinforce your memory.

Example: It's like practicing a musical instrument. The more you play, the better you get.

2. **Weekly Quizzes:** Take weekly quizzes to test your knowledge.

Example: Think of quizzes as your practice matches before the big game.

3. **Group Discussions:** Discuss current affairs with friends to deepen your understanding.

Example: Group discussions are like study jam sessions – collaborative and fun.

4. **Mock Tests:** Take mock tests to simulate the exam environment.

Example: Mock tests are like dress rehearsals for a play. The more you practice, the more confident you'll be on the actual day.

Keeping Track of Important Dates and Events

Important dates and events can be the difference between a good answer and a great one.

1. **Use a Calendar:** Mark important dates and events on a calendar.

Example: Think of your calendar as your event planner. It helps you remember key anniversaries and deadlines.

2. **Flashcards:** Use flashcards for quick revision of important dates and facts.

Example: Flashcards are like cheat sheets – quick, handy, and effective.

3. **Timeline Creation:** Create timelines for historical events and policies.

Example: Timelines are like road maps. They help you see the big picture and how events are interconnected.

Staying Balanced and Avoiding Burnout

Balance is crucial to avoid burnout and maintain peak performance.

1. **Regular Breaks:** Take regular breaks to rest and recharge.

Example: Think of breaks as pit stops in a race. They keep you going strong.

2. **Physical Activity:** Include physical activities in your routine to stay fit and energized.

Example: Exercise is like recharging your batteries. It boosts your energy and improves focus.

3. **Hobbies and Interests:** Engage in hobbies to relax and rejuvenate.

Example: Hobbies are like mental vacations. They help you unwind and come back refreshed.

4. **Healthy Diet:** Eat a balanced diet to keep your brain and body healthy.

Example: A healthy diet is like premium fuel for your car. It keeps your engine running smoothly.

Handling Information Overload

Managing the sheer volume of information can be challenging.

1. **Prioritize:** Focus on the most relevant and important news.

Example: It's like packing for a trip. Prioritize the essentials and leave out the rest.

2. **Filter Sources:** Choose quality over quantity when it comes to news sources.

Example: Think of it as curating a playlist. Only include the best tracks (news sources).

3. **Set Limits:** Limit your news intake to avoid getting overwhelmed.

Example: It's like setting screen time limits on your phone. Stay informed but not overloaded.

4. **Stay Organized:** Keep your notes and resources well-organized.

Example: Organization is like decluttering your workspace. It makes finding information easier and less stressful.

Making Learning Fun

Learning doesn't have to be boring. Make it enjoyable.

1. **Gamify Learning:** Turn learning into a game with quizzes and challenges.

Example: Treat it like a trivia night. The more you know, the more points you earn.

2. **Interactive Tools:** Use interactive tools like apps and websites for engaging learning.

Example: Interactive tools are like video games for your brain. Fun and educational.

3. **Storytelling:** Relate news to stories to make them more memorable.

Example: Think of each news story as an episode in an ongoing series. Engage with it like you would with a gripping TV show.

4. **Learning Groups:** Form study groups to make learning collaborative and fun.

Example: Study groups are like band practice. Everyone contributes, and the result is harmonious learning.

Conclusion: Your Roadmap to Mastering Current Affairs and General Knowledge

So there you have it, future IAS officers – your comprehensive, humorous guide to mastering current affairs and general knowledge. This journey is a marathon, not a sprint, but with the right strategies, a positive mindset, and a bit of humor, you can navigate it successfully.

1. **Stay Consistent:** Consistency is the key. Make news reading and revision a daily habit.

Example: Treat it like brushing your teeth. It's non-negotiable and essential.

2. **Stay Motivated:** Keep your end goal in sight. Visualize your success.

Example: Create a vision board with inspiring quotes, pictures of LBSNAA, and anything that keeps you motivated.

3. **Stay Positive:** There will be ups and downs. Stay positive and resilient.

Example: Think of yourself as Rocky Balboa – every setback is just a setup for a bigger comeback.

4. **Stay Balanced:** Balance your studies with relaxation and self-care.

Example: All work and no play makes Jack a dull boy. Don't forget to have some fun along the way.

With the right resources, a solid strategy, and a pinch of humor, you're all set to conquer the world of current affairs and general knowledge. So, go forth and show the world what you're made of. The road to LBSNAA is tough, but with determination and the right tools, you'll get there. Happy studying!

Ethics, Integrity, and Aptitude:

Welcome, future administrators! You've tackled history, geography, polity, and all the other heavyweight subjects. Now it's time to dive into the realm of ethics, integrity, and aptitude – the heart and soul of a good civil servant. This paper is like the moral compass guiding you through the maze of public service. Let's navigate this topic with a blend of humor, practical examples, and some good old-fashioned wisdom.

Understanding the Syllabus

First, let's break down what you need to know. The syllabus for this paper includes:

1. **Ethics and Human Interface:**

    o   Basic concepts and terminologies.

    o   Human values – lessons from the lives and teachings of great leaders, reformers, and administrators.

Example: Think of ethics as your internal GPS – guiding you on the right path even when you hit a moral traffic jam.

2. **Attitude:**

    o   Content, structure, function.

    o   Influence of attitude in thought and behavior.

    o   Moral and political attitudes, social influence, and persuasion.

Example: Attitude is like your smartphone's operating system. It influences how you process information and interact with the world.

3. **Aptitude and Foundational Values:**

    o   Integrity, impartiality, and non-partisanship.

    o   Objectivity, dedication to public service, empathy, tolerance, and compassion towards the weaker sections.

Example: These values are like the superpowers of a civil servant. Integrity is your shield, empathy is your healing touch, and dedication is your energy source.

4. **Emotional Intelligence:**

    o   Concepts and their utilities and application in administration and governance.

Example: Emotional intelligence is like being a Jedi. It's about understanding and managing your emotions and those of others.

5. **Contributions of Moral Thinkers and Philosophers:**

    o   From India and the world.

Example: Imagine a dinner party with Mahatma Gandhi, Socrates, and Confucius. Their wisdom helps shape your moral philosophy.

6. **Public/Civil Service Values and Ethics in Public Administration:**

    o   Status and problems.

    o   Ethical concerns and dilemmas in government and private institutions.

    o   Laws, rules, regulations, and conscience as sources of ethical guidance.

    o   Accountability and ethical governance.

Example: Public service values are like the rulebook of a game. They ensure fair play and guide your actions as a player in the governance arena.

7. **Probity in Governance:**

   o Concept of public service.

   o Philosophical basis of governance and probity.

   o Information sharing and transparency in government.

   o Right to Information, Codes of Ethics, Codes of Conduct, Citizen's Charters, Work Culture, Quality of Service Delivery, Utilization of Public Funds, and challenges of corruption.

Example: Probity is like the hygiene factor in a kitchen. Without it, everything else falls apart.

8. **Case Studies:**

   o Real-life examples to illustrate ethical dilemmas and solutions.

Example: Case studies are like your moral playground. They let you practice ethical decision-making in simulated scenarios.

Ethics and Human Interface

Ethics is like the inner voice that tells you right from wrong. Let's see how to navigate it.

1. **Basic Concepts and Terminologies:**

   o Understand terms like values, morals, ethics, and principles.

Example: Values are like the ingredients of a recipe. Morals are the recipe itself, ethics is the act of cooking, and principles are the guidelines that ensure the dish turns out well.

2. **Human Values:**

   o Lessons from great leaders.

Example: Mahatma Gandhi's honesty is like a beacon in a storm. It guides you when things get murky.

3. **Lessons from Lives and Teachings:**

- o   Learn from the experiences of great leaders.

Example: Nelson Mandela's resilience is like the strength of a mountain. It reminds you to stand firm even when the winds of adversity blow hard.

Attitude

Attitude shapes how we view the world and react to it. It's crucial for a civil servant.

1. **Content, Structure, Function:**

   - o   Understand the elements that form attitudes and how they influence behavior.

Example: Attitudes are like a pair of glasses. They color how you see the world – positive or negative.

2. **Influence of Attitude:**

   - o   How attitudes shape our thoughts and actions.

Example: A positive attitude is like having a sunny day mindset. It brightens everything around you.

3. **Moral and Political Attitudes:**

   - o   The impact of these attitudes on public service.

Example: Think of moral attitudes as the software updates that keep your ethical system running smoothly.

4. **Social Influence and Persuasion:**

   - o   How society and individuals influence our attitudes.

Example: Peer pressure is like a magnetic force. It pulls you in different directions, but a strong ethical core keeps you grounded.

Aptitude and Foundational Values

These values are the building blocks of a good civil servant.

1. **Integrity:**

- o Being honest and having strong moral principles.

Example: Integrity is like a lighthouse. It stands tall and guides you through the darkest of storms.

2. **Impartiality and Non-partisanship:**

   - o Treating everyone fairly without bias.

Example: It's like being a fair referee in a sports game. You call it as you see it, without favoring any side.

3. **Objectivity:**

   - o Making decisions based on facts and evidence.

Example: Objectivity is like a clear lens. It helps you see things as they are, not as you wish them to be.

4. **Dedication to Public Service:**

   - o Commitment to serving the public.

Example: Dedication is like a marathon runner's endurance. You keep going, no matter how tough the journey gets.

5. **Empathy, Tolerance, and Compassion:**

   - o Understanding and sharing the feelings of others.

Example: Empathy is like having a pair of magical glasses that let you see the world through others' eyes.

Emotional Intelligence

Emotional intelligence is your superpower in public service.

1. **Concepts and Their Utilities:**

   - o Understanding emotions and managing them effectively.

Example: Emotional intelligence is like being a mind reader. You understand not just what people say, but what they feel.

2. **Application in Administration:**

   o   Using emotional intelligence to improve governance.

Example: It's like being a skilled negotiator. You can navigate complex situations with tact and empathy.

Contributions of Moral Thinkers and Philosophers

Learn from the wisdom of the greats.

1. **From India and the World:**

   o   Study the teachings of moral thinkers and philosophers.

Example: Think of Aristotle's virtue ethics as a blueprint for building a good life. It's like having a moral GPS guiding you towards virtue.

2. **Applying Their Teachings:**

   o   Use their insights to shape your ethical framework.

Example: Confucius' emphasis on harmony and relationships can be like a guidebook for maintaining balance in public service.

Public/Civil Service Values and Ethics in Public Administration

These values form the core of your duties as a civil servant.

1. **Status and Problems:**

   o   Understand the current state and challenges in public service ethics.

Example: Think of it as diagnosing a patient. You need to know the symptoms (problems) to prescribe the right treatment (solutions).

2. **Ethical Concerns and Dilemmas:**

   o   Navigate the ethical challenges in government and private institutions.

Example: Ethical dilemmas are like tricky crossword puzzles. There's no easy answer, but with patience and thought, you can solve them.

3. **Laws, Rules, Regulations, and Conscience:**

   o   Sources of ethical guidance.

Example: These are like the user manuals for your ethical compass. They help you stay on the right path.

4. **Accountability and Ethical Governance:**

   o   Ensuring transparency and accountability.

Example: Accountability is like having a fitness tracker. It keeps you on your toes and ensures you meet your goals.

Probity in Governance

Probity is about integrity and uprightness in public life.

1. **Concept of Public Service:**

   o   Understanding the philosophical basis of governance.

Example: Public service is like being a gardener. You nurture and care for your community, ensuring it thrives.

2. **Philosophical Basis of Governance and Probity:**

   o   The underlying principles of ethical governance.

Example: Probity is like the foundation of a building. Without it, everything else crumbles.

3. **Information Sharing and Transparency:**

   o   The importance of openness in government.

Example: Transparency is like a clear glass window. It lets the light in and keeps things visible.

4. **Right to Information:**

- o   Empowering citizens through access to information.

Example: RTI is like having a magic key that opens doors to hidden information.

5. **Codes of Ethics and Conduct:**

   - o   Guidelines for ethical behavior.

Example: These codes are like a recipe for good governance. Follow them, and you'll create a healthy, functioning public service.

6. **Citizen's Charters and Work Culture:**

   - o   Ensuring quality service delivery and a positive work environment.

Example: Citizen's charters are like service guarantees. They promise and deliver quality public services.

7. **Challenges of Corruption:**

   - o   Tackling corruption in public service.

Example: Fighting corruption is like battling a hydra. Cut off one head, and another appears, but with perseverance, you can defeat it.

Case Studies

Case studies are practical applications of ethical principles.

1. **Real-Life Examples:**

   - o   Study real-life situations to understand ethical decision-making.

Example: Case studies are like virtual reality simulations. They let you experience ethical dilemmas without real-world consequences.

2. **Illustrating Ethical Dilemmas:**

   - o   Analyze how ethical principles are applied in complex scenarios.

Example: Think of case studies as choose-your-own-adventure books. Each decision leads to a different outcome.

Staying Balanced and Avoiding Burnout

1. **Regular Breaks:**

   o   Take regular breaks to rest and recharge.

Example: Think of breaks as pit stops in a race. They keep you going strong.

2. **Physical Activity:**

   o   Include physical activities in your routine to stay fit and energized.

Example: Exercise is like recharging your batteries. It boosts your energy and improves focus.

3. **Hobbies and Interests:**

   o   Engage in hobbies to relax and rejuvenate.

Example: Hobbies are like mental vacations. They help you unwind and come back refreshed.

4. **Healthy Diet:**

   o   Eat a balanced diet to keep your brain and body healthy.

Example: A healthy diet is like premium fuel for your car. It keeps your engine running smoothly.

Conclusion: Your Roadmap to Mastering Ethics, Integrity, and Aptitude

So there you have it, future IAS officers – your comprehensive, humorous guide to mastering ethics, integrity, and aptitude. This journey is a marathon, not a sprint, but with the right strategies, a positive mindset, and a bit of humor, you can navigate it successfully.

1. **Stay Consistent:**

   o   Consistency is the key. Make ethics and values a part of your daily life.

Example: Treat it like brushing your teeth. It's non-negotiable and essential.

2. **Stay Motivated:**

   o   Keep your end goal in sight. Visualize your success.

Example: Create a vision board with inspiring quotes, pictures of LBSNAA, and anything that keeps you motivated.

3. **Stay Positive:**

   o   There will be ups and downs. Stay positive and resilient.

Example: Think of yourself as Rocky Balboa – every setback is just a setup for a bigger comeback.

4. **Stay Balanced:**

   o   Balance your studies with relaxation and self-care.

Example: All work and no play makes Jack a dull boy. Don't forget to have some fun along the way.

With the right resources, a solid strategy, and a pinch of humor, you're all set to conquer the ethics paper. So, go forth and show the world what you're made of. The road to LBSNAA is tough, but with determination and the right tools, you'll get there. Happy studying!

Physical and Mental Well-being:

Alright, future IAS officers, you've been burning the midnight oil, hitting the books like there's no tomorrow. But guess what? It's not just about stuffing your brain with knowledge; you also need to take care of that amazing body and mind of yours. After all, what good is all that wisdom if you're too tired or stressed to use it?

The Importance of Physical Fitness

Imagine trying to drive a car with a flat tire. Not very efficient, right? Your body is the vehicle for your brain, so keeping it in top shape is crucial.

1. **Exercise Regularly:**

   o Regular exercise boosts your energy levels and keeps your mind sharp.

   o *Example*: Think of exercise as charging your phone. You wouldn't want to go into an important call (or exam) with 10% battery, would you?

2. **Types of Exercise:**

   o **Cardio:** Running, swimming, or cycling to get your heart pumping.

   o **Strength Training:** Lifting weights or doing bodyweight exercises like push-ups and squats.

   o **Flexibility:** Yoga or stretching to keep those muscles limber.

Example: Mix it up! Your exercise routine should be like a well-balanced meal – a bit of everything. Cardio is your main course, strength training is the side dish, and flexibility is the dessert.

3. **Stay Active Throughout the Day:**

   o Avoid sitting for too long. Take short breaks to move around.

   o *Example*: Imagine you're a squirrel – always on the move, gathering nuts (knowledge) but never sitting still for too long.

Nutrition: Fueling Your Brain and Body

You wouldn't put junk fuel in a Ferrari, right? Your body deserves premium nutrition to function at its best.

1. **Eat Balanced Meals:**

   o   Include a variety of fruits, vegetables, whole grains, and lean proteins.

   o   *Example*: Think of your plate as a rainbow. The more colorful your food, the better it is for you.

2. **Stay Hydrated:**

   o   Drink plenty of water throughout the day.

   o   *Example*: Water is like the oil in a machine. It keeps everything running smoothly. Plus, it helps you avoid those dreaded dehydration headaches.

3. **Limit Junk Food:**

   o   Treats are okay occasionally, but don't make them a habit.

   o   *Example*: Junk food is like that annoying friend who's fun in small doses but terrible in large quantities.

4. **Healthy Snacks:**

   o   Keep healthy snacks handy for when you need a quick energy boost.

   o   *Example*: Nuts, fruits, and yogurt are like the Avengers of snacks – powerful, reliable, and there to save the day.

Getting Enough Sleep

Sleep is like a magic potion for your brain. It restores, repairs, and rejuvenates.

1. **Stick to a Schedule:**

   o   Try to go to bed and wake up at the same time every day.

- o *Example*: Think of your body as a Swiss watch. It works best when it's well-regulated and consistent.

2. **Create a Sleep-Friendly Environment:**

   - o Keep your bedroom cool, dark, and quiet.

   - o *Example*: Your bedroom should be a cozy cave, perfect for hibernation.

3. **Avoid Screens Before Bed:**

   - o The blue light from screens can mess with your sleep.

   - o *Example*: Swap that late-night Netflix binge for a good book. Your brain will thank you.

4. **Relax Before Bed:**

   - o Establish a pre-sleep routine to wind down.

   - o *Example*: Think of it as a bedtime story for your brain. A warm bath, some light reading, or gentle stretches can help you drift off.

Managing Stress

Stress is like a bad WiFi connection. It disrupts everything and makes life difficult. Here's how to manage it.

1. **Practice Mindfulness:**

   - o Mindfulness helps you stay present and reduce anxiety.

   - o *Example*: Imagine you're a Jedi, calm and focused, using the Force to stay centered.

2. **Deep Breathing:**

   - o Deep breathing exercises can calm your mind and body.

   - o *Example*: Think of deep breathing as hitting the reset button on your brain.

3. **Take Breaks:**

   - Regular breaks can prevent burnout.

   - *Example*: Your brain is like a muscle. It needs rest between workouts to grow stronger.

4. **Stay Organized:**

   - Keeping your study space and schedule organized reduces stress.

   - *Example*: Imagine your brain as a filing cabinet. The more organized it is, the easier it is to find what you need.

Staying Mentally Fit

Mental fitness is just as important as physical fitness. Keep your brain in top shape with these tips.

1. **Engage in Hobbies:**

   - Hobbies are a great way to relax and recharge.

   - *Example*: Think of hobbies as mental vacations. They give your brain a break from the grind.

2. **Learn Something New:**

   - Challenge your brain with new skills or knowledge.

   - *Example*: Your brain is like a sponge. It loves soaking up new information.

3. **Socialize:**

   - Spend time with friends and family.

   - *Example*: Social interactions are like mental sparring sessions. They keep your mind sharp and engaged.

4. **Stay Positive:**

   - Maintain a positive outlook, even when things get tough.

- o *Example*: Think of yourself as a sunflower. Always look for the light, even on cloudy days.

Combining Study with Well-being

Balance is key to effective preparation. Here's how to blend study and well-being.

1. **Pomodoro Technique:**

   - o Study for 25 minutes, then take a 5-minute break.
   - o *Example*: It's like interval training for your brain. Work hard, then rest and recover.

2. **Active Breaks:**

   - o Use break time for physical activity or relaxation.
   - o *Example*: Do a quick workout, stretch, or dance like nobody's watching.

3. **Healthy Study Snacks:**

   - o Keep nutritious snacks handy while you study.
   - o *Example*: Think of snacks as brain fuel. Nuts, fruits, and veggies keep your energy levels stable.

4. **Mix Up Subjects:**

   - o Alternate between different subjects to keep your brain engaged.
   - o *Example*: It's like a well-rounded workout. Don't just focus on one muscle group.

Avoiding Burnout

Burnout is the enemy of productivity. Here's how to keep it at bay.

1. **Set Realistic Goals:**

   - o Break your study goals into manageable chunks.

- *Example*: Think of it as climbing a mountain. One step at a time gets you to the top.

2. **Reward Yourself:**

   - Celebrate small victories along the way.

   - *Example*: Treat yourself like a puppy learning new tricks. Small rewards keep you motivated.

3. **Know When to Stop:**

   - Recognize when you need a break and take it.

   - *Example*: It's like knowing when to fold in poker. Sometimes, you need to step back and recharge.

4. **Seek Support:**

   - Don't hesitate to ask for help if you're feeling overwhelmed.

   - *Example*: Think of support like a safety net. It's there to catch you when you fall.

Building a Support System

A strong support system can make all the difference.

1. **Stay Connected with Friends and Family:**

   - They can provide encouragement and perspective.

   - *Example*: Your support system is like your cheerleading squad. They keep you going.

2. **Join Study Groups:**

   - Collaborate with peers to stay motivated.

   - *Example*: Study groups are like team sports. Everyone works together towards a common goal.

3. **Mentors and Advisors:**

- o Seek guidance from teachers or mentors.

- o *Example*: Mentors are like wise old wizards. They offer wisdom and advice when you need it most.

4. **Use Online Communities:**

- o Participate in online forums and discussion groups.

- o *Example*: Online communities are like virtual coffee shops. Share ideas and get support from people all over the world.

Staying Motivated

Motivation is the fuel that keeps you going. Here's how to keep your tank full.

1. **Set Clear Goals:**

- o Know what you're working towards.

- o *Example*: Goals are like the finish line in a race. They give you something to strive for.

2. **Visualize Success:**

- o Picture yourself achieving your goals.

- o *Example*: Visualize yourself at LBSNAA, wearing that coveted IAS badge. Feels good, right?

3. **Stay Inspired:**

- o Read success stories and inspirational quotes.

- o *Example*: Inspiration is like a shot of espresso for your soul. It gives you a quick boost.

4. **Keep a Journal:**

- o Track your progress and reflect on your journey.

- o *Example*: Your journal is like a personal coach. It helps you see how far you've come and keeps you focused on your goals.

Managing Exam Anxiety

Exam anxiety is natural, but it can be managed.

1. **Prepare Thoroughly:**

    o   The better prepared you are, the less anxious you'll feel.

    o   *Example*: Preparation is like armor. It protects you from the slings and arrows of anxiety.

2. **Practice Relaxation Techniques:**

    o   Use techniques like deep breathing or meditation.

    o   *Example*: Think of relaxation techniques as your secret weapon. They help you stay calm under pressure.

3. **Stay Positive:**

    o   Focus on your strengths and achievements.

    o   *Example*: Positive thinking is like a superpower. It gives you the confidence to tackle any challenge.

4. **Seek Professional Help if Needed:**

    o   If anxiety becomes overwhelming, don't hesitate to seek help from a professional.

    o   *Example*: Professional help is like calling in the cavalry. Sometimes, you need extra support to win the battle.

Conclusion: Your Roadmap to Physical and Mental Well-being

So there you have it, future IAS officers – your comprehensive, humorous guide to maintaining physical and mental well-being. This journey is a marathon, not a sprint, but with the right strategies, a positive mindset, and a bit of humor, you can navigate it successfully.

1. **Stay Consistent:**

    o   Consistency is key. Make well-being a part of your daily routine.

- o *Example*: Treat it like brushing your teeth. It's non-negotiable and essential.

2. **Stay Motivated:**

   - o Keep your end goal in sight. Visualize your success.

   - o *Example*: Create a vision board with inspiring quotes, pictures of LBSNAA, and anything that keeps you motivated.

3. **Stay Positive:**

   - o There will be ups and downs. Stay positive and resilient.

   - o *Example*: Think of yourself as Rocky Balboa – every setback is just a setup for a bigger comeback.

4. **Stay Balanced:**

   - o Balance your studies with relaxation and self-care.

   - o *Example*: All work and no play makes Jack a dull boy. Don't forget to have some fun along the way.

Exam Day Strategies:

Alright, future IAS officers, the big day is finally here! It's time to put all those sleepless nights, endless cups of coffee, and stacks of books to the test. Think of the exam day as the grand finale of a talent show where you are the star performer. Let's walk through some exam day strategies with a generous dose of humor and practical examples to ensure you shine bright and score high.

Last-Minute Preparation Tips

Just like a chef does a final taste test before serving a dish, your last-minute preparation is all about fine-tuning.

1. **Revise Key Points:**

- o Go through your summaries and flashcards to refresh your memory.

- o *Example*: Imagine you're a detective reviewing your case notes before heading into the big interrogation.

2. **Avoid New Topics:**

- o Stick to what you already know. Last-minute cramming of new topics can lead to confusion.

- o *Example*: It's like trying to learn a new dance move right before a performance. You might trip and fall!

3. **Practice Breathing Exercises:**

- o Calm your nerves with some deep breathing or meditation.

- o *Example*: Think of it as being a Jedi mastering the Force. Stay calm, focused, and ready to conquer.

4. **Get a Good Night's Sleep:**

- o Ensure you get a full night's rest before the exam day.

- o *Example*: Treat sleep like charging your smartphone. You don't want to run out of battery in the middle of the day.

The Morning of the Exam

The morning of the exam is like the opening scene of a blockbuster movie – it sets the tone for the rest of the day.

1. **Eat a Healthy Breakfast:**

- o Have a nutritious meal to fuel your brain.

- o *Example*: Think of breakfast as your brain's power-up potion. Eggs, fruits, and whole grains can give you the energy boost you need.

2. **Dress Comfortably:**

- o Wear comfortable clothes that you can sit in for a long time.

- o   *Example*: Imagine you're dressing for a long flight. Comfort is key.

3. **Leave Early:**

   - o   Arrive at the exam center early to avoid any last-minute rush.

   - o   *Example*: It's like going to the airport. Better to be early and wait than to miss your flight.

4. **Carry Essentials:**

   - o   Double-check that you have all necessary items: admit card, ID, pens, and a watch.

   - o   *Example*: Treat your exam kit like a survival pack. Be prepared for anything!

Entering the Exam Hall

Stepping into the exam hall is like entering the gladiator arena. You need to be prepared, calm, and focused.

1. **Stay Calm and Positive:**

   - o   Keep a positive mindset. Believe in your preparation.

   - o   *Example*: Imagine you're a superhero about to save the world. Confidence is your superpower.

2. **Read Instructions Carefully:**

   - o   Pay attention to the exam instructions given by the invigilators.

   - o   *Example*: Treat instructions like a treasure map. They guide you to the prize (a good score).

3. **Organize Your Desk:**

   - o   Arrange your stationery neatly to avoid fumbling during the exam.

   - o   *Example*: Your desk is your battlefield. Keep your weapons (pens, pencils) ready for action.

During the Exam

The moment of truth! Here's how to tackle the paper like a pro.

1. **Read the Entire Paper First:**

    o   Quickly skim through all the questions before starting.

    o   *Example*: It's like scanning a menu before deciding what to order. Get an idea of what's on offer.

2. **Plan Your Time:**

    o   Allocate time for each section and stick to it.

    o   *Example*: Think of it as running a marathon with water stations (time checks) along the way. Pace yourself.

3. **Start with Easy Questions:**

    o   Answer the questions you're most confident about first.

    o   *Example*: It's like picking the low-hanging fruit. Easy wins boost your confidence.

4. **Manage Your Time:**

    o   Keep an eye on the clock and adjust your pace accordingly.

    o   *Example*: Imagine you're on a game show with a ticking timer. Keep track of time to avoid a last-minute rush.

5. **Stay Focused:**

    o   Avoid distractions and stay focused on your paper.

    o   *Example*: Think of yourself as a horse with blinders. Stay focused on the finish line.

6. **Review Your Answers:**

    o   If time permits, review your answers and make corrections.

- o *Example*: It's like proofreading an important email before hitting send. Ensure there are no silly mistakes.

Handling Tough Questions

Encountering a tough question is like hitting a roadblock. Here's how to navigate around it.

1. **Don't Panic:**

    - o Stay calm and don't let a tough question shake your confidence.

    - o *Example*: Think of it as facing a mini-boss in a video game. Stay calm, strategize, and tackle it step-by-step.

2. **Skip and Return:**

    - o If a question stumps you, move on and come back to it later.

    - o *Example*: It's like moving past a tricky level in a game. Clear the easier levels first and return with more power-ups.

3. **Elimination Method:**

    - o Use the process of elimination to narrow down multiple-choice options.

    - o *Example*: It's like playing "Who Wants to Be a Millionaire." Eliminate the wrong answers to improve your chances.

4. **Write Something:**

    - o For subjective questions, write something relevant. Partial credit is better than none.

    - o *Example*: Imagine you're a contestant on a cooking show. Even if the dish isn't perfect, presenting something is better than nothing.

Keeping Your Cool

Maintaining your composure is crucial for peak performance.

1. **Deep Breaths:**

- o Take deep breaths to stay calm.

- o *Example*: Think of deep breaths as your secret weapon. They help you reset and refocus.

2. **Positive Self-Talk:**

   - o Encourage yourself with positive thoughts.

   - o *Example*: Be your own cheerleader. "You've got this! You're prepared!"

3. **Stay Hydrated:**

   - o Drink water to stay hydrated and alert.

   - o *Example*: Water is like your brain's coolant. It keeps everything running smoothly.

4. **Avoid Comparisons:**

   - o Don't compare yourself with others during the exam.

   - o *Example*: It's like running your own race. Focus on your path, not the competitors'.

Post-Exam Routine

The exam is over. Now what?

1. **Relax and Unwind:**

   - o Take some time to relax and recharge.

   - o *Example*: Treat yourself to a movie, a good meal, or a nap. You've earned it!

2. **Avoid Post-Mortem:**

   - o Don't over-analyze the exam. What's done is done.

   - o *Example*: It's like not crying over spilled milk. Move on and focus on what's next.

3. **Prepare for the Next Paper:**

   - If you have more exams, shift your focus to the next one.

   - *Example*: It's like a multi-course meal. Enjoy one course at a time without worrying about the next.

4. **Stay Positive:**

   - Keep a positive mindset regardless of how you think you performed.

   - *Example*: Think of yourself as an optimist. Believe that you did your best and let it be.

Balancing Exam Days with Relaxation

Maintaining balance is key during exam season.

1. **Stick to a Routine:**

   - Maintain a regular routine to stay grounded.

   - *Example*: Think of your routine as a lighthouse. It guides you through the storm of exams.

2. **Engage in Light Activities:**

   - Engage in light physical activities or hobbies to relax.

   - *Example*: A short walk, some yoga, or listening to music can be like hitting the refresh button on your brain.

3. **Connect with Friends and Family:**

   - Spend time with loved ones to de-stress.

   - *Example*: Your support network is like your pit crew. They help you refuel and keep going.

4. **Stay Away from Negativity:**

   - Avoid negative thoughts or conversations about the exam.

- o *Example*: Think of negativity as a virus. Stay away to keep your mental health strong.

Visualizing Success

Visualizing success can boost your confidence and performance.

1. **Positive Visualization:**

   - o Visualize yourself succeeding in the exam.

   - o *Example*: Imagine yourself walking out of the exam hall with a big smile, knowing you did your best.

2. **Set Realistic Goals:**

   - o Set achievable goals for each exam.

   - o *Example*: Think of your goals as stepping stones. Each one gets you closer to your final destination.

3. **Reward Yourself:**

   - o Plan a reward for after the exams.

   - o *Example*: It's like promising yourself a treat after a hard workout. Motivation to keep pushing through.

4. **Affirmations:**

   - o Use positive affirmations to boost your confidence.

   - o *Example*: Repeat to yourself, "I am prepared, I am confident, I will succeed."

Conclusion: Your Roadmap to Exam Day Success

So there you have it, future IAS officers – your comprehensive, humorous guide to navigating exam day with confidence and poise. This journey is a marathon, not a sprint, but with the right strategies, a positive mindset, and a bit of humor, you can conquer the UPSC exams.

1. **Stay Consistent:**

- o Consistency is key. Stick to your preparation and exam day routines.
- o *Example*: Treat it like brushing your teeth. It's non-negotiable and essential.

2. **Stay Motivated:**

- o Keep your end goal in sight. Visualize your success.
- o *Example*: Create a vision board with inspiring quotes, pictures of LBSNAA, and anything that keeps you motivated.

3. **Stay Positive:**

- o There will be ups and downs. Stay positive and resilient.
- o *Example*: Think of yourself as Rocky Balboa – every setback is just a setup for a bigger comeback.

4. **Stay Balanced:**

- o Balance your studies with relaxation and self-care.
- o *Example*: All work and no play makes Jack a dull boy. Don't forget to have some fun along the way.

With the right resources, a solid strategy, and a pinch of humor, you're all set to conquer exam day. So, go forth and show the world what you're made of. The road to LBSNAA is tough, but with determination and the right tools, you'll get there. Happy studying and good luck!

Post-Examination Process:

Congratulations, future IAS officers! You've battled through the prelims, survived the mains, and conquered the interview. But hold your horses – the journey isn't over yet. The post-examination process is like the victory lap after a marathon. You still need to navigate through results, service allocation, and eventually, life at LBSNAA. Let's walk through this final stretch with humor and practical advice. (Let me tell you passing the medical exam, which usually happens one day after the interview, was most difficult. I will share the story in ethics classes.)

Understanding the Result Process

Waiting for results can feel like waiting for your favorite TV show's season finale – nerve-wracking and exciting.

1. **Patience is Key:**

     o   Results take time. Be patient and avoid constantly checking for updates.

     o   *Example*: Imagine waiting for your Hogwarts letter. It'll come when it's ready!

2. **Stay Updated:**

     o   Regularly check the official UPSC website for announcements.

     o   *Example*: Think of the UPSC website as your crystal ball – it's where you'll find all the important news.

3. **Avoid Rumors:**

- o Don't get swayed by rumors or false information.
- o *Example*: Gossip is like junk food – tempting but not good for you. Stick to reliable sources.

4. **Stay Positive:**

- o Keep a positive mindset while waiting for the results.
- o *Example*: Visualize your name on the merit list. Positive thoughts attract positive outcomes.

Life at LBSNAA

Welcome to LBSNAA – the Hogwarts for future bureaucrats! Here's what to expect and how to make the most of it.

1. **Training and Classes:**

- o The training at LBSNAA is rigorous and covers various aspects of public administration.
- o *Example*: Think of it as boot camp for your brain. Intense but incredibly rewarding.

2. **Physical Fitness:**

- o   Physical training is a key part of the curriculum.

- o   *Example*: Imagine a blend of military drills and yoga classes. It's all about building a strong body and mind.

3. **Networking:**

- o   Make connections with fellow officers from different services.

- o   *Example*: It's like building your own Avengers team. Diverse skills and backgrounds, united for a common cause.

4. **Extracurricular Activities:**

- o   Participate in various clubs and activities.

- o   *Example*: Join the debate club, cultural activities, or sports teams. It's like the extracurriculars in high school but way cooler.

5. **Field Visits:**

- o   You'll get to visit different parts of the country for practical training.

- o   *Example*: Think of it as a series of educational field trips. Learn by experiencing real-world scenarios.

Handling Post-Result Emotions

Whether you've made it to the list or missed it by a whisker, handling emotions post-results is crucial.

1. **Celebrate Your Success:**

- o   If you've made it, celebrate with friends and family.

- o   *Example*: Throw a party, have a cake, and dance like nobody's watching. You've earned it!

2. **Reflect and Plan:**

- o   If you didn't make it, take time to reflect and plan your next steps.

- *Example*: It's like missing a train. Another one will come. Use the waiting time to strategize your journey.

3. **Stay Positive and Resilient:**

   - Keep a positive outlook regardless of the outcome.

   - *Example*: Think of yourself as a phoenix. Rise from the ashes stronger than before.

4. **Seek Support:**

   - Talk to mentors, friends, and family for support.

   - *Example*: It's like leaning on your support crew during a marathon. They help you keep going.

Moving Forward: Preparing for Service

Once allocated, it's time to prepare for your service and the responsibilities it brings.

1. **Understand Your Role:**

   - Research your specific role and responsibilities.

   - *Example*: Think of it as reading the manual before using a gadget. Know what's expected of you.

2. **Brush Up Skills:**

   - Enhance skills relevant to your service.

   - *Example*: If you're joining the police service, improve your fitness and legal knowledge.

3. **Connect with Seniors:**

   - Reach out to seniors in your service for guidance.

   - *Example*: It's like getting tips from experienced players before joining a new team.

4. **Stay Informed:**

   - Keep up with current affairs and developments related to your service.

   - *Example*: Stay updated like a news anchor. Know what's happening in your field.

Making the Most of LBSNAA

LBSNAA is not just about training; it's also about personal growth and building lifelong friendships.

1. **Embrace the Experience:**

   - Dive into the training with enthusiasm and an open mind.

   - *Example*: Treat it like an adventure camp. Every activity is a new learning experience.

2. **Build Relationships:**

   - Form bonds with your batchmates. These connections will last a lifetime.

   - *Example*: Think of it as building your own network of superheroes. Stronger together.

3. **Participate Actively:**

   - Engage in all activities and make the most of every opportunity.

   - *Example*: Join clubs, lead projects, and take initiatives. It's like participating in a treasure hunt. Every clue (activity) leads to a new discovery.

4. **Reflect and Grow:**

   - Use this time to reflect on your goals and personal growth.

   - *Example*: It's like a personal retreat. Learn more about yourself and your aspirations.

Preparing for Real-World Challenges

LBSNAA prepares you for the real-world challenges of public service. Here's how to gear up.

1. **Practical Skills:**

   o   Focus on acquiring practical skills that will help you in the field.

   o   *Example*: It's like learning to ride a bike. You need both theory and practice.

2. **Adaptability:**

   o   Be ready to adapt to different environments and situations.

   o   *Example*: Think of yourself as a chameleon. Adaptability is your superpower.

3. **Problem-Solving:**

   o   Hone your problem-solving skills through simulations and case studies.

   o   *Example*: It's like solving puzzles. The more you practice, the better you get.

4. **Leadership and Teamwork:**

   o   Develop your leadership and teamwork abilities.

   o   *Example*: Be a team player and a leader. It's like being the captain of a sports team.

Life Beyond LBSNAA

Graduating from LBSNAA is just the beginning. Here's what to expect as you step into the real world of public service.

1. **On-the-Job Training:**

   o   Your first posting will be a learning experience.

- o *Example*: Think of it as an internship. You'll learn the ropes on the job.

2. **Challenges and Opportunities:**

   - o Be prepared for challenges and seize opportunities to make a difference.

   - o *Example*: It's like a video game. Every level has new challenges and rewards.

3. **Continuous Learning:**

   - o Keep learning and improving your skills throughout your career.

   - o *Example*: Treat your career as a lifelong learning journey. There's always something new to learn.

4. **Making an Impact:**

   - o Remember why you joined the service and strive to make a positive impact.

   - o *Example*: You're the superhero in this story. Use your powers for good and make a difference.

Staying Grounded and Humble

No matter how successful you become, staying grounded and humble is crucial.

1. **Remember Your Roots:**

   - o Never forget where you came from and what motivated you to join the service.

   - o *Example*: It's like a tree. No matter how tall it grows, it's grounded by its roots.

2. **Serve with Integrity:**

   - o Always uphold the values of integrity and honesty.

- o *Example*: Think of integrity as your moral compass. It keeps you on the right path.

3. **Give Back:**

   - o Use your position to give back to society and help those in need.

   - o *Example*: It's like being a mentor. Share your knowledge and help others grow.

4. **Stay Connected:**

   - o Maintain connections with your peers and mentors.

   - o *Example*: Your network is like a safety net. It supports you through thick and thin.

Celebrating Milestones

Celebrate your achievements and the milestones along the way.

1. **Small Wins:**

   - o Celebrate small victories and milestones.

   - o *Example*: It's like collecting trophies in a game. Every win counts.

2. **Big Achievements:**

   - o Celebrate major achievements with your loved ones.

   - o *Example*: Throw a party, share your success, and enjoy the moment.

3. **Reflect and Plan:**

   - o Reflect on your journey and plan your next steps.

   - o *Example*: Think of it as plotting your course on a map. Every milestone is a waypoint on your journey.

4. **Stay Grateful:**

   - o Be grateful for the opportunities and support you've received.

- o *Example*: Gratitude is like the sunshine that helps you grow. Appreciate the journey and those who've helped you along the way.

Conclusion: Your Roadmap to the Post-Examination Journey

1. **Stay Consistent:**

   - o Consistency is key. Stay focused on your goals and keep moving forward.

   - o *Example*: Treat it like brushing your teeth. It's non-negotiable and essential.

2. **Stay Motivated:**

   - o Keep your end goal in sight. Visualize your success.

   - o *Example*: Create a vision board with inspiring quotes, pictures of LBSNAA, and anything that keeps you motivated.

3. **Stay Positive:**

   - o There will be ups and downs. Stay positive and resilient.

   - o *Example*: Think of yourself as Rocky Balboa – every setback is just a setup for a bigger comeback.

4. **Stay Balanced:**

   - o Balance your studies with relaxation and self-care.

   - o *Example*: All work and no play makes Jack a dull boy. Don't forget to have some fun along the way.

Balancing UPSC Preparation with Personal Life:

Hello, future IAS officers! So, you're on this incredible journey to become a top-notch civil servant. But hey, life isn't just about studying all day and night, right? You've got friends, family, hobbies, and maybe even a Netflix account waiting for you. Balancing UPSC preparation with personal life can seem like walking a tightrope, but with a bit of humor and some practical tips, you can master it. Let's dive into how you can juggle both without dropping the ball.

The Art of Time Management

Time management is like making a perfect cup of tea – you need the right ingredients and timing.

1. **Create a Schedule:**

   o   Plan your day with time slots for study, relaxation, and personal activities.

   o   *Example*: Think of your schedule as a well-balanced meal. Too much of one thing isn't healthy.

2. **Prioritize Tasks:**

   o   Identify your most important tasks and tackle them first.

   o   *Example*: It's like eating your veggies before dessert. Get the essential stuff done first.

3. **Use Productivity Techniques:**

   o   Techniques like the Pomodoro Technique (25 minutes study, 5 minutes break) can be effective.

   o   *Example*: Imagine studying in sprints rather than a marathon. Quick bursts followed by short breaks keep you fresh.

4. **Avoid Procrastination:**

   o   Stay disciplined and avoid delaying tasks.

   o   *Example*: Procrastination is like a leaky faucet. A little drip here and there, and before you know it, the sink is overflowing.

Integrating Personal Life and UPSC Preparation

Your personal life doesn't have to take a backseat while preparing for UPSC. It's all about integration.

1. **Combine Study with Fun:**

    o   Mix your study sessions with enjoyable activities.

    o   *Example*: Listen to a podcast on current affairs while going for a walk. It's like killing two birds with one stone.

2. **Stay Social:**

    o   Spend quality time with friends and family.

    o   *Example*: Think of your social interactions as energy boosters. They recharge you for your next study session.

3. **Healthy Lifestyle:**

    o   Eat well, exercise, and get enough sleep.

    o   *Example*: Treat your body like a high-performance car. It needs the right fuel and maintenance to run smoothly.

4. **Hobbies and Interests:**

    o   Don't give up on your hobbies. They provide a great way to relax.

    o   *Example*: Hobbies are like dessert after a meal. They add sweetness to your life.

Setting Realistic Goals

Setting realistic goals ensures you don't burn out while keeping your progress on track.

1. **Short-term Goals:**

    o   Break down your big goals into smaller, manageable tasks.

- o *Example*: It's like eating an elephant one bite at a time. Manageable chunks make it doable.

2. **Reward Yourself:**

   - o Celebrate small victories to stay motivated.

   - o *Example*: Think of rewards as checkpoints in a video game. They keep you motivated to reach the next level.

3. **Adjust as Needed:**

   - o Be flexible and adjust your goals as needed.

   - o *Example*: If you're running a marathon and hit a wall, adjust your pace rather than stopping altogether.

4. **Stay Positive:**

   - o Maintain a positive mindset even when things get tough.

   - o *Example*: Think of yourself as a rubber band. Flexible and resilient, bouncing back from setbacks.

Handling Stress and Pressure

Stress and pressure are inevitable, but managing them effectively is key to staying on track.

1. **Mindfulness and Meditation:**

   - o Practice mindfulness or meditation to stay calm.

   - o *Example*: Think of meditation as hitting the reset button on your brain. A few minutes can make a huge difference.

2. **Breaks and Relaxation:**

   - o Take regular breaks to relax and rejuvenate.

   - o *Example*: Breaks are like pit stops in a race. They help you refuel and continue stronger.

3. **Talk it Out:**

   o   Share your concerns and stresses with friends or family.

   o   *Example*: Talking about your worries is like airing out a stuffy room. It clears the air and makes you feel better.

4. **Stay Active:**

   o   Physical activity can reduce stress and improve focus.

   o   *Example*: Exercise is like a magic pill. It boosts your mood and energy levels.

Efficient Study Techniques

Make the most of your study time with efficient techniques.

1. **Active Learning:**

   o   Engage actively with the material through discussions and practice.

   o   *Example*: Active learning is like cooking a meal rather than just reading the recipe. It sticks better.

2. **Note-Making:**

   o   Make concise and effective notes for quick revision.

   o   *Example*: Good notes are like a well-organized toolkit. Everything you need is at your fingertips.

3. **Mock Tests:**

   o   Regularly take mock tests to assess your progress.

   o   *Example*: Mock tests are like dress rehearsals for a play. They prepare you for the real performance.

4. **Study Groups:**

   o   Join or form study groups for collaborative learning.

- o *Example*: Study groups are like group workouts. More fun and motivating than going solo.

Staying Motivated

Staying motivated throughout the long preparation period is crucial.

1. **Visualize Success:**

   - o Imagine yourself achieving your goals.
   - o *Example*: Visualize yourself at LBSNAA, wearing that coveted IAS badge. It's a powerful motivator.

2. **Inspiration from Success Stories:**

   - o Read about other successful candidates to stay inspired.
   - o *Example*: Success stories are like fuel for your motivational engine. They keep you going.

3. **Daily Affirmations:**

   - o Use positive affirmations to boost your confidence.
   - o *Example*: Affirmations are like pep talks. "I am capable, I am focused, I will succeed."

4. **Balance and Fun:**

   - o Keep your life balanced with fun activities.
   - o *Example*: Fun activities are like the seasoning in a dish. They make the whole experience enjoyable.

Avoiding Burnout

Burnout can derail your preparation, so it's important to avoid it.

1. **Recognize the Signs:**

   - o Know the signs of burnout, such as constant fatigue and lack of motivation.

- o *Example*: Burnout signs are like warning lights on your car dashboard. Don't ignore them.

2. **Take Time Off:**

   - o Don't hesitate to take a break if you feel overwhelmed.

   - o *Example*: Taking time off is like rebooting your computer. It helps resolve issues and improve performance.

3. **Diversify Activities:**

   - o Mix up your routine with different activities.

   - o *Example*: Diversifying your activities is like a balanced diet. It keeps you healthy and engaged.

4. **Seek Help:**

   - o Talk to mentors, friends, or professionals if needed.

   - o *Example*: Seeking help is like calling tech support. Sometimes, you need expert advice to solve problems.

Creating a Supportive Environment

A supportive environment can make a huge difference in your preparation.

1. **Family Support:**

   - o Involve your family in your journey and seek their support.

   - o *Example*: Family is like your home base. They provide stability and comfort.

2. **Peer Support:**

   - o Surround yourself with positive and motivated peers.

   - o *Example*: Motivated peers are like training partners. They push you to perform better.

3. **Mentorship:**

- o Find a mentor who can guide you through the process.

- o *Example*: A mentor is like a GPS. They help you navigate the ups and downs of the journey.

4. **Positive Environment:**

- o Create a study space that is conducive to learning.

- o *Example*: A good study space is like a greenhouse for plants. It helps you grow and thrive.

Maintaining Mental Health

Your mental health is as important as your physical health.

1. **Mindfulness Practices:**

- o Incorporate mindfulness practices into your daily routine.

- o *Example*: Mindfulness is like decluttering your mind. It helps you focus better.

2. **Limit Screen Time:**

- o Avoid excessive screen time to reduce stress.

- o *Example*: Limiting screen time is like giving your eyes a vacation. It helps reduce strain.

3. **Healthy Boundaries:**

- o Set boundaries to balance study and personal time.

- o *Example*: Boundaries are like fences. They keep your work and personal life separate.

4. **Stay Connected:**

- o Stay connected with loved ones for emotional support.

- o *Example*: Emotional support is like a safety net. It catches you when you fall.

Conclusion: Your Roadmap to Balance

So there you have it, future IAS officers – your comprehensive, humorous guide to balancing UPSC preparation with personal life. This journey is demanding, but with the right strategies, a positive mindset, and a bit of humor, you can navigate it successfully.

1. **Stay Consistent:**

   o   Consistency is key. Keep moving forward, no matter what.

   o   *Example*: Treat it like brushing your teeth. It's non-negotiable and essential.

2. **Stay Motivated:**

   o   Keep your end goal in sight. Visualize your success.

   o   *Example*: Create a vision board with inspiring quotes, pictures of LBSNAA, and anything that keeps you motivated.

3. **Stay Positive:**

   o   There will be ups and downs. Stay positive and resilient.

   o   *Example*: Think of yourself as Rocky Balboa – every setback is just a setup for a bigger comeback.

4. **Stay Balanced:**

   o   Balance your studies with relaxation and self-care.

   o   *Example*: All work and no play makes Jack a dull boy. Don't forget to have some fun along the way.

Maintaining Motivation Throughout the UPSC Journey:

Hello, future IAS officers! Buckle up because we're about to dive into the wild ride of maintaining motivation throughout your UPSC journey. Think of it as being the protagonist in a never-ending superhero movie where the villain is procrastination, and your superpower is unyielding motivation. Let's explore this epic saga with humor, practical tips, and a bit of fun.

The Hero's Call to Action

Every epic journey starts with a call to action. For you, it's the decision to take on the UPSC challenge.

1. **Why Did You Choose UPSC?**

    o   Reflect on your reasons for choosing UPSC.

    o   *Example*: It's like remembering why you decided to train like a Jedi – the thrill, the challenge, and the ultimate goal of becoming a guardian of peace (or public service).

2. **Set Clear Goals:**

    o   Define your short-term and long-term goals.

    o   *Example*: Think of it as plotting your route on a treasure map. Each goal is an X marking a spot to reach.

3. **Visualize Success:**

    o   Picture yourself as an IAS officer, making a difference.

    o   *Example*: Visualizing success is like watching the climax of your favorite superhero movie. You're the hero saving the day.

4. **Create a Mission Statement:**

    o   Write a personal mission statement to remind you of your purpose.

    o   *Example*: Your mission statement is like a superhero's motto – "With great power comes great responsibility."

Building Your Superpower: Consistency

Consistency is your superpower. It's what keeps you going even when the going gets tough.

1. **Daily Routine:**

    o   Establish a daily routine that balances study, rest, and play.

    o   *Example*: Your routine is like Batman's utility belt – packed with everything you need to tackle the day.

2. **Study Schedule:**

    o   Create a study schedule and stick to it.

    o   *Example*: Think of your schedule as a time-turner from Harry Potter. It helps you manage your time effectively.

3. **Break It Down:**

    o   Break down your study material into manageable chunks.

- o *Example*: It's like slicing a giant pizza into pieces. Easier to handle and more enjoyable.

4. **Regular Breaks:**

- o Take regular breaks to avoid burnout.

- o *Example*: Breaks are like the intermissions in a movie. They give you time to relax and recharge.

The League of Mentors

Every hero needs a mentor. Someone who guides, motivates, and provides wisdom.

1. **Find a Mentor:**

- o Seek out mentors who have successfully navigated the UPSC path.

- o *Example*: Your mentor is like Dumbledore to Harry – wise, supportive, and full of useful advice.

2. **Join Study Groups:**

- o Join or form study groups for mutual support and motivation.

- o *Example*: Study groups are like the Avengers – different strengths coming together to achieve a common goal.

3. **Online Forums and Communities:**

- o Participate in online forums and communities for advice and motivation.

- o *Example*: Think of these forums as virtual Hogwarts – a place to share knowledge and support each other.

4. **Regular Feedback:**

- o Get regular feedback on your progress from mentors or peers.

- o *Example*: Feedback is like a mirror. It helps you see where you stand and what needs improvement.

Battling the Villains: Procrastination and Distraction

Procrastination and distraction are the villains you need to defeat.

1. **Identify Distractions:**

   o Identify what distracts you and find ways to eliminate or manage them.

   o *Example*: Distractions are like the Joker – sneaky and disruptive. Keep them at bay with focus and determination.

2. **Set Boundaries:**

   o Set boundaries for your study time to avoid interruptions.

   o *Example*: Boundaries are like the Bat-Signal – a clear sign that you're in serious mode.

3. **Use Productivity Tools:**

   o Use apps and tools to stay focused and organized.

   o *Example*: Productivity tools are like Iron Man's suit – high-tech aids that boost your efficiency.

4. **Reward Yourself:**

   o Reward yourself for completing tasks to stay motivated.

   o *Example*: Rewards are like the cookies after saving the world. Small treats that keep you going.

Keeping the Flame Alive: Inspiration and Motivation

Staying inspired is crucial. Here's how to keep that motivational flame burning.

1. **Inspirational Stories:**

   o Read about successful UPSC candidates and their journeys.

   o *Example*: Inspirational stories are like the origin stories of superheroes – they remind you that anything is possible.

2. **Daily Affirmations:**

   - Use daily affirmations to boost your confidence and motivation.

   - *Example*: Affirmations are like Captain America's shield – they protect you from negativity and self-doubt.

3. **Visualize Your Success:**

   - Spend a few minutes each day visualizing your success.

   - *Example*: Visualization is like seeing the end credits of your movie – it reminds you of the happy ending you're working towards.

4. **Create a Vision Board:**

   - Create a vision board with images and quotes that inspire you.

   - *Example*: Your vision board is like the Batcave – a place filled with reminders of your mission and goals.

Staying Balanced: The Importance of Self-Care

Even heroes need to rest and take care of themselves.

1. **Exercise Regularly:**

   - Incorporate physical activity into your daily routine.

   - *Example*: Exercise is like training at the X-Mansion. It keeps you fit and ready for any challenge.

2. **Healthy Diet:**

   - Eat a balanced diet to fuel your body and mind.

   - *Example*: A healthy diet is like the elixir of life – it keeps you energized and focused.

3. **Adequate Sleep:**

   - Ensure you get enough sleep every night.

- o *Example*: Sleep is like recharging your superpowers. Essential for peak performance.

4. **Relaxation Techniques:**

- o Practice relaxation techniques like meditation or deep breathing.
- o *Example*: Relaxation techniques are like using the Force – they help you stay calm and focused.

Embracing Failures: Learning from Setbacks

Setbacks are part of the journey. Embrace them and learn from them.

1. **Accept Failures:**

- o Accept that failures are part of the learning process.
- o *Example*: Failures are like plot twists in your story – unexpected but essential for character development.

2. **Analyze Mistakes:**

- o Analyze your mistakes and learn from them.
- o *Example*: Mistakes are like detective clues. They help you understand what went wrong and how to fix it.

3. **Stay Resilient:**

- o Stay resilient and keep pushing forward.
- o *Example*: Resilience is like Wolverine's healing factor. It helps you recover and keep fighting.

4. **Celebrate Progress:**

- o Celebrate your progress, no matter how small.
- o *Example*: Progress celebrations are like the post-credits scenes in Marvel movies – small victories that keep the excitement alive.

Finding Your Passion: The Fuel for Motivation

Passion is the fuel that keeps your motivation engine running.

1. **Identify Your Passion:**

   o   Identify what you're passionate about within the realm of public service.

   o   *Example*: Your passion is like the Philosopher's Stone – it gives you unlimited motivation and drive.

2. **Align Goals with Passion:**

   o   Align your study goals with your passion.

   o   *Example*: Aligning goals with passion is like finding the perfect spell – it makes everything easier and more enjoyable.

3. **Engage in Passion Projects:**

   o   Engage in projects related to your passion during breaks.

   o   *Example*: Passion projects are like side quests in a game. They keep things interesting and fun.

4. **Stay Curious:**

   o   Stay curious and keep learning about your areas of interest.

   o   *Example*: Curiosity is like Hermione's Time-Turner – it allows you to explore new dimensions of knowledge.

Staying Connected: The Importance of Community

Being part of a community provides support and motivation.

1. **Study Groups:**

   o   Join or form study groups for mutual support.

   o   *Example*: Study groups are like the Fellowship of the Ring – a team united by a common goal.

2. **Online Communities:**

- o Participate in online forums and communities.
- o *Example*: Online communities are like the Jedi Council – a place to share wisdom and seek guidance.

3. **Family and Friends:**

- o Stay connected with family and friends for emotional support.
- o *Example*: Family and friends are like Alfred to Batman – always there to support you.

4. **Networking:**

- o Network with peers and professionals in your field.
- o *Example*: Networking is like attending the Hogwarts Yule Ball – an opportunity to meet and connect with others.

The Final Battle: Exam Day Strategies

The exam day is your final battle. Prepare well and stay calm.

1. **Stay Calm:**

- o Practice deep breathing and stay calm on the exam day.
- o *Example*: Staying calm is like using the Force – it keeps you focused and centered.

2. **Time Management:**

- o Manage your time effectively during the exam.
- o *Example*: Time management is like a Quidditch match – every second counts.

3. **Read Instructions Carefully:**

- o Read the exam instructions carefully before starting.
- o *Example*: Instructions are like a treasure map – they guide you to your goal.

4. **Stay Positive:**

   - Maintain a positive mindset throughout the exam.
   - *Example*: Positivity is like a Patronus charm – it wards off negative thoughts and fears.

Celebrating Victory: The End of the Journey

Once the exams are over, take time to celebrate your hard work and dedication.

1. **Reflect on the Journey:**

   - Reflect on your journey and the progress you've made.
   - *Example*: Reflecting is like watching a movie montage – seeing all the hard work and growth.

2. **Celebrate Your Efforts:**

   - Celebrate your efforts with friends and family.
   - *Example*: Celebrating is like the final battle victory party – well-deserved and joyous.

3. **Plan for the Future:**

   - Plan your next steps, regardless of the outcome.
   - *Example*: Planning for the future is like mapping out sequels for your superhero saga.

4. **Stay Grateful:**

   - Stay grateful for the support and opportunities you've had.
   - *Example*: Gratitude is like the heart of a superhero – it keeps you grounded and humble.

Conclusion: Your Epic Journey to Motivation

So there you have it, future IAS officers – your comprehensive, humorous guide to maintaining motivation throughout your UPSC journey. This journey is demanding, but with the right strategies, a positive mindset, and a bit of humor, you can navigate it successfully.

1. **Stay Consistent:**

   o   Consistency is key. Keep moving forward, no matter what.

   o   *Example*: Treat it like brushing your teeth. It's non-negotiable and essential.

2. **Stay Motivated:**

   o   Keep your end goal in sight. Visualize your success.

   o   *Example*: Create a vision board with inspiring quotes, pictures of LBSNAA, and anything that keeps you motivated.

3. **Stay Positive:**

   o   There will be ups and downs. Stay positive and resilient.

   o   *Example*: Think of yourself as Rocky Balboa – every setback is just a setup for a bigger comeback.

4. **Stay Balanced:**

   o   Balance your studies with relaxation and self-care.

   o   *Example*: All work and no play makes Jack a dull boy. Don't forget to have some fun along the way.

With the right resources, a solid strategy, and a pinch of humor, you're all set to maintain your motivation like a true hero. So, go forth and show the world what you're made of. The road to LBSNAA is tough, but with determination and the right tools, you'll get there. Happy studying and stay motivated!

<u>**YOU WANT TO KNOW MORE, You can reach me here....**</u>

Whatsapp Number : 8800021111

Email : <u>Prince1991L@gmail.com</u>

Telegram : @Prince_Luthra

Youtube: Prince Luthra IAS 2.0 and Netmock 2.0